would be tender for a few days, but I . . . .
Maybe I should go the doctor. It's hard to be patient.

"Those who wait on the Lord will renew their strength" (but when you're waiting and weary, it's hard to be patient). James writes, "Be patient, therefore, brethren until the coming of the Lord. Behold the farmer waits for the precious fruit of the earth, being patient over it until it receives the early and the late rain. You also be patient. Establish your hearts...." Establish your hearts. James instructs us to allow God to do what God does — to send the early and the late rain — and to wait upon what God will do, expecting precious fruit.

Steven Covey in his highly acclaimed *Seven Habits of Highly Effective People* discusses the productive practice of having a time of idea planting, growth and development, and harvesting. He recommends a focus on things which are "important," and resisting the dominance of the "urgent." Things which are important include such things as building relationships, exercising, writing a personal mission statement, long range planning, preventative maintenance, preparation — "all those things we know we need to do, but somehow we seldom get around to doing because they aren't 'urgent.'"[1] Establish the heart, James writes. Make plans, form intentions in normal times to establish the heart. If we are patient, if we wait on the Lord (and focus on the important) in the ordinary days, then in the demanding seasons of planting and harvesting and in the precarious time of storm and darkness we will have hearts prepared and established enough to persevere.

Sometimes it is hard to be patient as a parent. Count to ten, sit on the sofa with a child, and discuss what happened. What went wrong? Why was it dangerous? Give the child an alternative, go to another room, start a new activity and sometimes the best decision for a parent is simply to walk away. With a little thought, whatever it is may not seem to be that important.

Sometimes it is hard to be patient as a parent ... but patience isn't always hard. And when patience is richly available, parents can plan to lead gently. Make a plan ahead of time to lead our children gently so we will know what to do in the midst of our frustration, tiredness, disappointment, and confusion.

Sometimes it's hard to be patient in a marriage — establish the heart when patience is richly available. Take the Marriage Encounter quiz.[2] Answer each question yes or no. "My spouse and I never have any trouble communicating (yes or no). When I make my spouse angry, I always know why (yes or no). I always know when my spouse is interested in making love (yes?). My spouse and I always agree on child-rearing techniques (?). My spouse and I are perfectly matched as far as sexual needs and desires (?). Work, TV, sports, children, and family never interfere with my ability to talk with or be with my spouse (?)." Is it hard to be patient even with your spouse? Establish your heart when patience is richly available.

However, when patience is worn thin, we travel through an emotional black hole where the familiar seems strange. We stumble in our homes as if in darkened rooms with the furniture in disarray. James' voice whispers, "The Lord is coming soon." This is precisely the time when our hearts are greatly opened to his coming.

The ancient Jewish parable tells of Baal Shem-Tov, the great rabbi who loved his people. If he sensed his people were in danger, he would depart to a place in the woods near a great tree, light a special fire, and say a mysterious prayer. And always without exception, the people he loved would be saved from danger. Magid of Mezritch became leader after Baal Shem-Tov passed on. As his teacher before him, whenever Magid sensed a danger for the people, he would go to a place in the woods near a great tree. He would say, "Dear Lord, I do not know how to light the special fire, but I know the mysterious prayer. Please let that be good enough." And it was, and the people were always saved from danger. The Rabbi Moshe-leib of Sasov came to lead the people when Magid passed on. And each time he heard the people were in danger, he would go to the place in the woods near the great tree. He would say, "Dear Lord, I do not know how to make the special fire, I do not know the mysterious prayer, but I know the place in the woods near this great tree. Please let this be good enough." And it was and the people were always saved from danger. Rabbi Israel of Rizhyn came to lead the people when Rabbi Moshe passed on and whenever the people were in danger, he didn't even get out of his armchair. He shrugged his shoulders and could only bow his head and pray, "Dear Lord, I do not know how to make the special fire. I do not know the mysterious prayer. I cannot find my way to the place in the woods near the great tree. All I know is the story, please let this be good enough." And it was, and his people were always saved.[3]

Dear Lord, sometimes when we are greatly challenged, greatly in need, in deep darkness, we forget the special place in the woods and sometimes even to pray. Be patient with us, as we patiently wait for You. For in these times we remember the story and out of deep darkness, You send a messenger to us, saying, "Behold I bring you good news of a great joy which will be to all the people, to every one of you. Behold I bring *you* good news of great joy." Dear Lord: Be patient with us as we patiently wait for You.

---

1. Steven Covey, *Seven Habits of Highly Effective People* (New York: Simon and Schuster, 1989), p. 154.

2. The complete quiz can be found on the Wichita, Kansas, Marriage Encounter web site, E-mail address: texan@southwind.net. For more information contact World Wide Marriage Encounter at 1-800-795-5683.

3. This is an adaptation of a story found on Dell Doughty's Internet Story Page (February 1997). Address: www.huntcol.edu/~ddoughty/fabula.html.

Designated Son Of God

Romans 1:1-7

"**Descended** from David ... designated Son of God in power according to the Spirit of holiness ..." so Paul writes of the One who is to come; the One we are expecting (Romans 1:3, 4); the designated Son of a designated God come to a designated people. God reveals himself in power; we humbly and imperfectly place names on what we see and feel. God designates a Son and the Son designates a people.

Designating/Naming

What we know of our world and of God is as human as life itself. From the beginning of time we have been naming. Frederick Buechner describes his favorite teacher, Old Testament professor James Muilenburg. Muilenburg's popular Intro to Old Testament course was held in the largest lecture hall at Union Theological Seminary. Students brought their friends and those friends brought friends until the place was standing room only. Striding about the lecture hall, as Buechner describes it, he was a professor who "never merely taught the Old Testament but was the Old Testament. He would be Adam, wide-eyed and halting as he named the beasts — 'You are ... an elephant ... a butterfly ... an ostrich!' " — Adam naming, and we have been naming ever since.[1]

We have named this season "Advent." It is a time of preparation, of expectancy. The Bible says that the birth of Jesus came at God's appointed time. God set the time and we named it. It is little wonder that in the time of year when days are shortest and when we long for the coming of the light, Jesus is born and we name him the Light of the World.

In all kinds of ways we name this season "Holy." Cedar evergreens remind us of the royalty of Christ: Christ the King. With its sharp points and red berries, holly, even in the midst of our festivity, foreshadows the crucifixion. And the hard candy shaped for a shepherd's staff turned on its head becomes a "J" for Jesus; added to its rock of ages hardness is a red stripe because his blood was shed for the sins of the world, thinner red stripes for the stripes he received from the Roman soldiers and sometimes a green stripe to remind us that Christ is a gift from God.

So God comes into the world in revelation, powerful and true, and we name what we see.

Think of Moses standing on a hillside, a fugitive from Egypt, tending his father-in-law's sheep. There is a bush which burns but is not consumed. Moses stands transfixed at the site. "Moses, Moses, take off your shoes for the ground on which you stand is holy ground." And Moses falls on his face, for no one can look upon the face of God and live. "What shall I call you? By what name will you be known?" Moses asks.

"I am who I am."

"How will I know how to find you?"

"I will be with you. In the wilderness I will lead you: a pillar of smoke by day and at night a pillar of fire."

When we stand in the presence of God, we take off our shoes; we fall on our faces. We receive a name which is too holy to be spoken, so we wrap words around its edges: Rock of Ages, cleft for me; Infant holy, Infant lowly; Mighty God, Wonderful Counselor, Everlasting Father, Prince of Peace. We think of Rock, Refuge, Fortress, Shield, Refiner, Purifier, Shepherd, Judge, King. It is true that the One who caused that bush to burn on a hillside long ago is divine and in the earliest of times his name was considered too holy to pronounce at all — YHWH.

So two millennia ago, those who were wise looked into the heavens and followed what they saw there, traveling west, sensing God was about to do something new — a new revelation from the

One we have received and named. *"God With Us* in a new way," the designated Son of God.

How Are We Designated?

So, how are we designated; how are we chosen? People are chosen all the time: chosen to walk on the moon, to sing the national anthem on opening day, to bake the cake, to host the party; chosen for adoption; chosen to read the Christmas story.

Many would recognize Boomer Esiason as a quarterback in the National Football League, but not many would know Cheryl, his wife. Cheryl and Boomer know that some children seem to be chosen differently. In 1993 Boomer and Cheryl Esiason established the "Heroes Foundation" after their son Gunnar was diagnosed with a fatal genetic disorder — cystic fibrosis.

> *When children such as Gunnar have been chosen to go into a battle at such an early age, it is not because they are being punished or cursed by God. It is because they are a gift; an inspiration. They are here to challenge us to open our eyes to life's frailties, its contingencies and just how precious it is. They are here to teach us — they are our heroes."* — Cheryl Esiason[2]

So God decided to do something new: to send his Son and to name him, much as we name our children. He sent the long expected One in an unexpected way. God sent his Son and designated him Emmanuel, Savior, Shepherd.

Have you ever named someone? When we were expecting our children, as is always the case with expectant parents, we asked the challenging question: What shall we name him? Names having to do with faith, family, and friends, we thought. The name needed to have just the right sound — considering the last name with which the child would be saddled, a simpler name with fewer syllables seemed fitting. We quickly eliminated some of the mulitsyllabic biblical favorites: Aminadab, Josaphat, Ezekias, and Jechonias.

For our first son: Joseph — the name of a friend's son who had died too young and the name of Jesus' earthly father; Richard —

the name of both my wife's father and mine. And for our *second* son it seemed self-evident that we should give him the name which means "First Man" and David — the name of a wonderful friend and Israel's greatest king. Elizabeth would have joined us had Adam been a girl, which might have led to our having two "Beths" or a "Betsy" or how about "Liz Luchsinger"?

When Jesus was to be born, the attention of his earthly parents turned to his naming. God made it easier for them by directly providing his name, which is about the only way being the parent of Jesus turned out to be easier than being the parent of an average child. And when God gave Jesus his name, God chose a name, "Jesus," which was a common name among the people of Mary and Joseph's community; a common name for an uncommon baby who through his life would take the common and, in a miracle of transformation, create "the best wine," "bread enough to feed the multitude with fish also" and transform "a broken loaf and a cup into a holy presence" and "a wooden tool of execution into a symbol of life and hope." Jesus, named by God, designated Son, lived up to his designation and to his name.

The Son Designates Others

So God decided to do something new and brought the long-expected One into the world in an unexpected way. His parents were commoners and transient, and soon would be the focus of hostility. And yet he brought hope, and yet he *was* hope. Of course, this is but the beginning of his story. The designated Son of God comes into the world and designates others. A woman by the well is designated through forgiveness, the blind are made to see, the hungry on the hillside are fed, the lost are found. The designated Son of God comes into the world to designate others and calls them at the seaside from their nets or in the street from collecting taxes. He calls them from their grief, illness, and greed to life abundant in love for God and others. So the designated Son designates others, designates us as his dearly beloved, the sheep of his pasture, his flock, his friends, the ones for whom he lays down his life.

And so we designate him Mighty God, Wonderful Counselor, Prince of Peace. Then the wonderful love of the designated Son places on our hearts a wonderful love for God's people, and we find ourselves on roads we would not have traveled, in endeavors we would not have pursued, in benevolences which we would not have otherwise found appealing. The designated Son does not send us forth on a forced march, but rather sends us *as those who have found freedom*, to see as he would see, to speak as he would speak, to heal as he would heal, and to love as he would love.

So our God, whose name is a vessel of holiness, designated a Son and he designated others, designated *us*. Would you have expected anything else? And what do you expect in this season of expectancy? Or when do you expect it? Jill Dakota tells of a dream-like winter walk on a starry, dark night, very cold, following a path illuminated by red lanterns.

> *Out of a grove of evergreens as it was beginning to snow, a woman in a red cape and very pregnant, with long golden braids, came to take my arm; to a little log cabin she led me. Tired, we wrapped ourselves in quilts and sat near a blazing fire, drank spiced cider, and laughed like children. I felt cared for and warm like scarcely I could remember. The woman smiled at me radiantly and began to undo her yellow braids. I threw another log on the fire. At last I asked, "Is your baby due soon?"*
>
> *And she, with a calm, expectant smile answered, "Oh yes, very soon."[3]*

Our God designates a Son and he designates others, designates *us*. Would we have expected anything else? And what do we expect in this season of expectancy? And when do we expect it? Is *The Baby* due soon; our Baby? And what shall we name him? What will *you* name him when he draws near? — Jesus, shepherd, savior, friend? Are we *soon and very soon* expecting the One who Was, and Is, and Is To Come?

Come, Lord Jesus, be our guest; bless what Thou has given us. O designated Son of God, your name is holiness. In the advent of your coming, designate us by your love. Call us from our nets at the seaside; from the streets of collecting treasure. Call us from our grief, our greed, our idleness, and illness to life abundant in your love. Designate us as your dearly beloved, the sheep of your pasture, your flock, your friends, the ones for whom you lay down your life.

---

1. Frederick Buechner, *Now and Then* (San Francisco: Harper and Row, 1983), p. 15.

2. Cheryl Esiason, *Heroes Foundation* (www.heroes.com/sheriff.htm).

3. Jill Dakota, *Yule* (members.aol.com/JillDakota/yule.htm).

Hoofs, Paws, And Christmas Pause

Titus 2:11-14

"The grace of God has appeared ... training us ... to await our blessed hope" (Titus 2:11-13), and oh, how we have waited! The air is filled with anticipation, the Holy Night has come. We each wait for different things: the lighting of candles, the singing of carols, loved ones returning home, feasting, and forgetting ferment, for the Prince of Peace is coming. We wait for delight in the eyes of someone we love as he or she opens that special gift. We wait in awe in the hope that *one star's strong light lingers still* and will lead us home to him who redeems us.

And we have weathered a season of starlight and storm, of commercialism and community, of frustration and fraternity, of decoration, delicacy, department stores, and devotion. Congratulations, you've made it.

Not so long ago a father of two young girls had almost made it to this moment. Maximum household excitement had stretched patience beyond what is wise. The girls were given the opportunity to play "quietly" in their room as evening fell. The two girls in one room had forgotten the "quietly" in the parental instruction and a tidal wave of enthusiasm again threatened equilibrium in the house.

"Tap, tap, tap." (Silence) "Tap, tap, tap." (Silence) Quick to the window, two sets of eyes peer over the windowsill into the darkness. In the next bedroom their father quickly pulls in through an open window an extended arm and mop handle.

"He has come checking!" The girls squeal.

"How do you know?" their father asks.

33

"We heard him tap on the window and look there — tracks of his sleigh in the snow and reindeer hoofs." The surprised dad looks out at what might be reindeer tracks and sleigh marks in the snow, or evidence that the neighbor boy took a short cut home after sledding. Who's to say? *Congratulations. You've made it!*

He Comes To Reclaim Our Value

We await our blessed hope, the One who comes to redeem us — to reclaim our value.

To us, who are in danger of being valueless because of the way we have devoted ourselves, because of the things we have pursued, because of the way we have fought with one another, because of the way we have been distracted, dismayed, disappointed, and disheartened, right now, at this time, he comes to reclaim our value and gives us the greatest gift — the gift of himself.

But in this season he is not the only one who comes. Have you ever heard, "Dress the Christmas cat" or been told to wear a new garment for Christmas, lest you get "caught by the Christmas cat"? A centuries-old Icelandic legend reports that there is a gargantuan and sinister Christmas cat who is ready to wreck havoc on lazy humans. In Icelandic villages work on the autumn wool is an imperative and consuming endeavor. If you didn't do your part, you received the double disappointment — missing out on the reward of a new article of clothing and becoming a tasty treat for the Christmas cat. In this season, also come those things which "eat up" our thought, our attention, our energy, our calm, our pause. They come from around the edges of the season — lists of things to do, people to greet, parties to attend, and the One who has redeemed us is sacrificed again. But not this year for there is still time to find our Christmas Pause.

"The grace of God has appeared ... training us ... to await our blessed hope," and as we wait, light recaptures us, shining from a strong and steady star; the voice of an angel, a song barely more than silence, brushes the ear. We listen ... listen. Christmas Pause.

Harriet Lewis Bradley, more than a hundred years ago, wrote a beautiful story of two childhood playmates at Christmas time — Elizabeth Joy and Sidney St. John. Elizabeth was cast to be the angel in the Christmas tableau, and Sidney promised to make for his friend flowing angel wings to wear with her costume. Returning home from a trip to distant relatives, Sidney, aboard an ocean transport, is delayed by mechanical failure on board ship, angel wings boxed and ready for Elizabeth in his possession. Finally he arrives home to find that Elizabeth Joy has succumbed to a sudden illness, not violent but devastating. While Sidney's ship, still at sea, "drifted onward, from a quiet room a girl's soul also drifted, drifted in some way to somewhere, and it was all in the night."[1]

So Sidney St. John arrived home carrying a box of angel wings. He found the family seated in a room around the fire with a small portrait of a child, "Elizabeth Joy, aged ten," upon which the light of a swinging lamp fell, nearby a Christmas tree decked, ready to light. Because of his days at sea, to return home to find his playmate gone was not thoroughly strange, but what seemed stranger was that the people about him were living and were expecting to live. He was in dream-like observation — distanced, people coming and going, children passing, scene by scene as if in a play.

Very late in the evening, the house had grown still, and Sidney St. John returned to the room. He took the small portrait of "Bessie" from the wall and sat with it in his hands — sat like one who would never dream, nor wish, nor hope again.

But then he sensed a presence in the room. He could see clearly every object by the light of the lamp above his head. And yet there was a presence and he sensed it. "He could not tell how he perceived the presence; only that it stood under the Christmas tree; that it wore neither butterfly wings nor wings long and sweeping. It was simply Elizabeth as he had been accustomed to see her, and so natural seemed the circumstance of her appearance that it caused no feeling of any unusual occurrence."[2] And then it went away and Sidney St. John replaced on the wall the picture of Elizabeth Joy. He extinguished the light of the swinging lamp, and with a sense of sweet, sweet comfort, left the room.

"The grace of God has appeared ... training us ... to await our blessed hope." Tonight we Pause. Waiting, listening for the sound of the One who is coming; who bridges heaven and earth and reclaims us. Is he coming — as he said he would? Will he join us in our Christmas Pause? Will we see his footprints or those of another? "Let all mortal flesh keep silence, and with fear and trembling stand; ponder nothing earthly minded...." The grace of God has appeared and trained us ... to await our blessed hope, to await the One who gave himself for us to redeem us — to return to us our worth. Christmas Pause.

---

1. Harriet Lewis Bradley, *The Christmas Angel* (December 1894), www.theatlantic.com/unbound/flashbks/xmas/chrintro.htm, p.

2. *Ibid.*

We Know Exactly
How You Feel, Jesus

Hebrews 2:10-18

Oh, Christmas has come and gone, but its scent lingers: spiced cider, evergreen, bayberry candles, cookies baking, popcorn, ham and scalloped potatoes, chestnuts roasting, and hot chocolate. Christmas has come, and its scent lingers: the aroma of newspaper casually read by a crackling fire or the smell of a new book received as a gift; pungent chemicals of instant pictures developing, or tempera paint on a homemade gift; play-dough, silly putty, gift perfume or cologne, shoe polish applied generously for a Christmas Eve shine. Christmas has come and its scent lingers.

In this season of angels, Paul proclaims that it is not with the angels that Christ is concerned but with men and women — children of Abraham. "For surely it is not with angels that he is concerned, but with the descendants of Abraham. Therefore he had to be made like his brethren in every respect, so that he might become a merciful and faithful high priest in the service of God ..." (Hebrews 2:16, 17). Did he have to become Love Incarnate and be "made like his brethren in every respect" so that he could understand us? Or so that we could understand him?

A youth choir at a church was in rehearsal preparing a pageant which included some upbeat songs and choreography. One of the regulars in the group, Melissa, had brought a friend who was not catching on to the rhythm or the words. As sometimes happens, the regular had become focused on her own preparation and had forgotten about shepherding her friend. Also in the group was a boy named Cash Box because he always seemed to have money in his pocket, which won him favor with some. His social

37

awkwardness and offensive banter, however, usually left his interpersonal balance sheet in the negative. As the rehearsal continued, Melissa's friend became more and more embarrassed, feeling clumsy and out of place. Finally she broke from the group. Down the hallway she fled, trying not to be noticed, pretending to read a bulletin board, flushed with tears, mortified, wishing she had never come. Soon footsteps approached from behind. It was Cash Box. The youth pastor edged closer to the scene, concerned over what Cash might say. "Hey, I saw you in there. Don't worry, this song's kinda hard; don't really know it myself. But we can't learn it standing out here. C'mon, let's go back in. You won't be alone. I know what it's like to be alone."

Sometimes we wonder: Do you know I'm alone, Jesus? Do you know exactly how I feel? Jesus taught that God cares for the lilies of the field and the birds of the air and that the hairs on our head are numbered in God's eyes. But how can we know God understands? That Christ understands?

Because he became like us in every respect. He became like us in every respect ... that he might become merciful and faithful in the service of God. And ... he knows how we feel because he reaches out with a healing touch.

The Sunday school hymn "He Touched Me" was inspired by the many gospel stories of *Jesus' healing touch.* After the Sermon on the Mount, Jesus came down from the mountain, as great crowds followed him. And he was approached by a leper who said, "Lord, if you will, you can make me clean" (Matthew 8:2) and Jesus stretched out his hand saying, "Be clean." And immediately the man's leprosy was cleansed.

Likewise as Jesus approached the city of Nain, Jesus and his disciples came upon the corpse of a dead man being carried from the city. He was the only son of his mother and she was a widow. Jesus passed through the large crowd accompanying the burial procession. And when he saw the widow, he had compassion and said to her, "Do not weep." And Jesus came and touched the bier and said, "Young man, I say to you, arise." And sitting up, the dead man began to speak (Luke 7:11-15).

Likewise a woman who for a dozen years searched for healing from a flow of blood came up behind Christ, and *she touched him,* touching his garment's fringe, and immediately the flow of blood ceased (Luke 8:43, 44). He touched the one who could not hear and could not speak. He touched the one born blind and he touched the children and blessed them.

But study these Bible stories and we learn that "touched" would more correctly be translated "held or grasped." He *held* the man with leprosy and *holding* him said, "Be clean." He *grasped* the one who was blind; he *grasped* the one who was born without hearing and could not speak. He *held* the children and blessed them. The woman with a twelve-year flow of blood *grasped* him, *held* him, and he said, "Take heart, daughter, your faith has made you well." Jesus, do you know how I feel? "Yes, my child, for I have touched you, held you, and I will hold you again."

But we are sometimes more like the child in a department store who absentmindedly reaches for a parent's hand and mistakenly grasps the hand of another, walking with the stranger a few steps then staring up with shock and astonishment at a surprised and unfamiliar face. We also absentmindedly take the hand of one who will lead us. Sometimes we walk hand in hand for an extended time until, on pathways severe and threatening, we look up startled to see we have taken our lead not from the Lord but from another. Or like Peter trying to traverse threatening water, losing his faith, beginning to sink, our voice cries out, "Lord, save me!"

"I have held you before and I will hold you again." We hear his words as he stops our sinking and pulls us back to life.

In this week at the close of the year, it is not unusual to feel that we have occasionally been led by a hand other than his hand down paths which he would not choose. So it is fitting to ask as the year draws to a close, "In the year to come, by whose hand will we be led; whose hand will we hold?" In this time after your birth, Jesus, we also ask, "How do you feel?" We want to touch you and be in touch with you. We want to hold you.

In that time long ago in the town of Jesus' birth a few came to witness and bless him at his nativity: shepherds, potentates, a few unnamed others. Did they, before they returned to their fields and flocks, and before they returned to their distant country by another way, bend to hold him? Did they lift him or stoop to touch him? Oh, what a moment in a shepherd's life to cradle the King of Glory! What a moment in your life and mine!

A few years ago a small church was hosting homeless families at Christmastime. It was nearly bedtime as the pastor wandered the hallways of the church in casual attire, visiting with the resident guests and volunteer hosts. He stopped at the church kitchen, which was often a gathering place, and found a dad just done drying his one-year-old son, softly patting him dry after a bath in the deep stainless steel sink. "Here, could you hold him for a moment?" he said, handing the pastor the towel-wrapped boy. "I'll be right back. I need to get his pajamas." Oh, how precious were his dark eyes and little hands. The pastor swayed gently with the little fellow as the babe reached up and felt the rough whiskers on the pastor's late-in-the-evening chin. He smells just like my son, he thought, just like God's son.

Oh, God, did you need to come into the world, did Jesus need to come so that you could understand us? (You know already how many hairs we have on our heads.) Or did you come, did he come so that we could understand you? Did he come so that he could hold us or did he come so that we could hold him?

And he was made like his brothers and sisters in every respect that he might become a merciful and faithful high priest in the service of God.

And if we held you, Jesus, how would you feel? Would you feel our love and devotion, our faithfulness and gentle care? Would you feel secure and well placed in our arms or pleased in the beginning time of your life? Oh, Lord, in these days, even in these times, how can we hold you in our love? Help us to receive well the ones who are placed in our hands and in our lives. Help us to value them and with listening hearts to comfort and calm. Let the children come, regardless of chronological age, and may it be as in the days of old, when you said, you were hungry and we fed thee, naked and we clothed thee, sick and imprisoned and we visited thee ... new in the world ... and we held thee. When we have done it to one of the least of these, you said, we have done it to thee.

Yes, we know
exactly how you feel, Jesus,
when we hold thee.
We also know your fragrance.

Oh, Christmas has come
and the aroma
of Christ
lingers.

Just In Time

Ephesians 1:3-14

A plane flies through the night. A winter storm howls as the pilot radios for meteorological information, trying to steer clear of the worst of it. All has gone well apart from the weather. The news that a *heart* was coming had reached the airport in plenty of time for the pilot to ready her plane for take off. By the time the ambulance arrived with sheriff escort, the engines were warm and ready to taxi onto the runway. The controller held air traffic as the two-engine craft sped down the runway and lifted into the air.

But now the weather: Will she be able to complete her route? "Continue ahead," comes the report, "but landing may be a problem." An hour and a half passes, more bad weather. The controller at the receiving airport decides to bring her in with the caution, "Low visibility, some icing on the runway." A bumpy but uneventful landing accomplished, the plane taxis to an ambulance waiting on the tarmac. The heart loaded, two police cars and an ambulance speed away, lights flashing. With the heart incoming from the airport, surgery can begin at University Hospital. Timing is important. Shortly, the patient will be ready to receive his new heart, just in time.

Paul suggests that from the beginning of time some were destined to understand the mystery of God's will according to his purpose which he set forth in Christ. Paul and others were first to understand the mystery and power of Christ. Then came others and after them others still. And after many, many more, we came, seeking to understand the same mystery and the same power which God revealed in the fullness of time in Jesus. Through the many centuries the people waited and in God's time in the fullness of time, just in time, Jesus was born. Just in time for Paul, just in time for Peter and James and John, just in time for Mary Magdelene and Zacchaeus, just in time for Nicodemus, Mary and Martha and Lazarus, just in time for you and for me.

Consider another winter scene: a different time and place. Armies are on the move. In one last desperate attempt to reassert the strength and strategic position of the Third Reich, Field Marshall Gerd Von Rundstedt initiates a winter offensive which history later named The Battle of the Bulge. In Von Rundstedt's path lies a small Belgian crossroads known as Bastogne, a road junction vital to German progress. The One Hundred and First Airborne is surrounded. Brutal winter conditions increase the challenge as soldiers wrap their faces in woolen scarves, becoming almost indistinguishable to one another. The scene becomes increasingly hopeless. German command offers the One Hundred and First the opportunity to surrender. At this, General Anthony McCallough answers the Von Runstedt demand with one word, a response which will long live in military lore. "Nuts!" he writes on a piece of paper, handing it to the German courier. Later, with supplies running low and conditions failing to improve, Lt. Colonel Creaton Abrams' Thirty-Seventh Tank Battalion breaks through bringing relief to the One Hundred and First — just in time.[1]

Or consider a space mission attempting to land on the moon. Two astronauts in a lunar lander thirteen hundred feet above moon dust. Looking out triangular windows, Neil Armstrong and Buzz Aldrin prepare to land — Neil will soon take over from the computer and fly the lander while Buzz backs up man and machine.

"Ah!" Neil exclaims. The lander, running out of fuel, has overshot the landing zone by four miles and is heading straight for a yawning, boulder-filled crater. There is no gliding in space to conserve fuel, a lander is nothing but dead weight in a vacuum. "Ninety seconds ... Seventy-five seconds ... Sixty seconds," Aldrin calls out the amount of fuel remaining. The slow descent continues as the cool test pilot/astronaut Armstrong searches for a flat place. Someone in Mission Control half whispers, "You'd better remind them that there are no darn gas stations on the moon." "Thirty seconds.".... There! A spot where the rocks are thinning out. Aldrin continues calling numbers as the *Eagle* Lunar Lander eases toward the moon. Finally, the historic words from Armstrong, "Houston, Tranquillity Base here. The *Eagle* has landed." At 4:17 p.m. EDT, July 20, 1969, the first humans landed on the moon *with sixteen seconds of fuel remaining* — just in time.[2]

Or consider a young Hebrew who has been challenged by God to bring God's people out of bondage. He has been arguing with the leaders of Egypt for some time, and finally by signs and wonders has convinced Pharaoh to free the Hebrews from slavery to depart peacefully. However, after the Hebrew departure has begun, Pharaoh has second thoughts and sends his army to track them down. Now pursued and traveling in haste, Moses and the people are trapped at the Red Sea and Pharaoh's army is closing in fast. At God's instruction, Moses raises his hand over the water. God separates the water with a strong east wind and the people of Israel cross over on dry land — just in time.

Or consider a young virgin who is being raised by a Jewish uncle because her parents are dead. A call goes out from the king to search 127 provinces to find a replacement for his "fallen out of favor" queen. This young virgin is pleasing to the king and he brings her into his court. But there is a catch: one of the king's most trusted advisors has grown to hate the Jews and desires to have them destroyed. And edict has already gone out with the king's authority to eliminate the Jews from the provinces. How can this young queen speak on behalf of her people? Such an attempt most certainly will earn her the same fate as the last queen, possibly worse. Her uncle, Mordecai the Jew, reminds her that her life and those of all of her people are in serious jeopardy.

"Think not that in the king's palace you will escape any more than all the other Jews. For if you keep silence at such a time as this, relief and deliverance will rise for the Jews from another quarter, but you and your father's house will perish," he says. "And who knows whether you have not come to the kingdom for such a time as this?" Esther instructs Mordecai in reply, "Go, gather all the Jews ... and hold a fast on my behalf, and neither eat nor drink for three days, night or day. I and my maids will also fast as you do. Then I will go to the king, though it is against the law; and if I perish, I perish" (Esther 4:13-16). So Esther went to the king and over a series of days revealed to him the plot against her people which brought even the king's chosen queen to grave danger. He listened to Esther and was persuaded by her. Thus, the king replaced his order of destruction against the Jews with an order of protection, because a queen had courage and risked herself on behalf of her people — just in time.

Or consider Jesus, baptized by John.
He lifted the dead to life,
broke the loaves and fish to feed a multitude,
calmed the sea, cast out demons,
preached in the synagogue, ate with sinners,
blessed little children, challenged his church,
died on a cross,
and was raised to life on the third day —
just in time.

Literature, film, and history are filled with just-in-time reinforcements, rescues, changes of fortune. We now have a widely accepted manufacturing strategy called "just in time" because materials and parts arrive at the factory "just in time for production." Thus, manufacturers do not have capital tied up in warehouses full of that which is waiting to be processed.

Often we pray to a "just in time" God. We desire for our benevolent God to send healing, hope, manna in the desert, rain on the parched earth, peace, prosperity, guidance and direction, all "just in time."

And when healing does come, when help arrives, when our position is clarified and direction is found, sometimes we have the presence of mind to pray thankful prayers to the One who is the source of life and love.

However, when hope and help still seem far off, when rain does not come in its season, when the hungry are left with little, we are prone to grumble. Remembering the parable of the workers in the vineyard: Jesus tells the story of the land owner who goes to the market place to find workers for his vineyard. He travels repeatedly,

46

hiring some at the beginning of the day, some in the middle, and some nearly at the end of the day. The benevolent landowner, when the work is done, pays each the same. All, except for those hired at the end of the day, grumble because especially those who have come very late in the day have been paid so generously.

And when we pray to our "just in time" God, and God sends help and healing just in time to others rather than to ourselves, we grumble. Some may say, "But we have heaped prayers high to heaven. Why has God not honored us?"

But to understand God thus is to miss the picture, purpose, and power of Christ. Paul suggests that some understood first the mystery and power of his will. "We who first hoped in Christ have been appointed to live for the praise of his glory." Others came next and then many, many more, until even we have heard the word of truth, the gospel of our salvation, and have believed in him.

But we do not believe he will without exception come to rescue us, arriving just in time. For it has always been true of believers; there are some things from which we cannot be rescued or will not be rescued.

As we begin the last year before the turn of the millennium, we have already been hearing plenty about the end of time, the return of Christ, the cosmic significance of this mark in time. And one thing from which we will not be rescued is the eventual ending of our time as living, breathing persons on this earth. No matter how you look at it, we *are* running out of time and the end of time for us is coming. Maybe we will go out collectively together, but it will be more likely as someone has written, "We will each slip away quietly, one at a time, while the party is still going strong." In a real sense the end is near for all of us. Some will go sooner than others and the timely arrival upon which we all depend is the One we celebrate in this season of the year, in this second Sunday of Christmastide. You see, the rescue upon which we depend happened in advance; we were reinforced prior to our very beginning, and our prayers were heard before they were ever said. So it is not as if God must arrive just in time to save us. God was here, is here, and will be here to save us, and the conclusion of our story is already assured in a beautiful way.

So the significant cosmic event in time which makes all the difference for you and for me is our estimated time of arrival in the unfolding story of the kingdom. And how in the coming year will our arrival again in The Story be different than in the past? Paul writes, "You also have heard the word of truth and the gospel of your salvation, you have believed in him which is the guarantee of your inheritance." In this coming year, let us live with confidence as heirs, as thankful beneficiaries of the love of One who arrived and who will arrive in the fullness of time.

---

1. Based on events as described by Walter Cronkite, *A Reporter's Life* (New York: Knopf, 1996), pp. 120 ff.

2. Allan Shepherd and Deke Slaton, *Moonshot* (Atlanta: Turner Publishing, 1994), pp. 21-29.

Sermon Series:
Moving At The Speed Of Light

Introduction

Light travels at 186,000 mi/sec, and over short distances the speed of light is virtually instantaneous. But if radio signals (traveling at the speed of light) are sent from the moon or Mars to Earth, we observe a delay between the sending and receiving moments. Thus light, as fast as it is, takes time to travel.

This is true of The Light of the World as well. Through the incarnation, God chose to cast The Light in human form and make its traveling subject to the challenges of this world. The Light has not "instantaneously" traveled to all portions of the globe; in fact it takes a while, once it has entered the human soul, to reflect and refract until it has entered all portions of the person's being.

So, what is the speed of Light?
How does Light travel?
Where did Light travel in the time of Jesus and his
followers?
And where does Light travel in our lives?

Through this season of Epiphany we will take up these questions. In just a few sermons, this is not intended to be an exhaustive study, but a jumping-off point for further reflection. We will use as a frame of reference places to which Jesus and his followers traveled, and link biblical places with places of crucial importance in our lives. I hope you enjoy this journey with The Light and that The Light always shines well on your path.

— FL

Moving At The Speed Of Light

Ephesians 3:1-12

At the end of Matthew's gospel, Jesus instructs his disciples: "All authority in heaven and on earth has been given to me. Go therefore and make disciples of all nations, baptizing them in the name of the Father and of the Son and of the Holy Spirit, teaching them to observe all that I have commanded you; and lo, I am with you always, to the close of the age" (Matthew 28:16-20). Once again, the Light is on the move.

How does light move? Differently, depending on its courier. One can imagine a party of explorers in a darkened cave with miners' helmets shining, or a water craft's navigation lamps quietly passing in the night, or a black forest with the searching beams of rescuers seeking a lost child — *Light on the move* as it has always been since Jesus walked the paths of Galilee.

How Does The Light Move?

The speed of Light in those days was a walking pace. Jesus walked almost everywhere. Sometimes he traveled by boat and he took at least one short and famous ride on a colt. He walked as did others in his community — his parents, siblings, and neighbors. When Jesus was a baby, his family fled to Egypt, a two-week trek. When Mary and Joseph annually traveled to Jerusalem to celebrate the Passover, they prepared for a five-day walking journey. When Jesus and his followers set out from Nazareth to Jericho, the trip was expected to take four or five days.

In his ministry, Jesus was always on the move visiting towns in Galilee: Cana, Na'in, Tiber'ias, Magdala, Capernaum; and around

Jerusalem: Bethany, Jericho, Bethphage. He encouraged others to be on the move as well.

In Luke, he appoints seventy and sends them ahead of him, instructing them to carry no purse, no bag, no sandals, and to eat what the locals provide. If upon entering a town its residents receive the disciples, they are to heal the sick in that place and proclaim, "The kingdom of God has come near to you" (Luke 10:1-12).

So it is no surprise that as the Gospel of Matthew concludes, Jesus commands his disciples, "Go, make disciples of all nations...." The Light is on the move and his disciples will be couriers of the Light.

Paul: Courier Of The Light

Paul knew this assignment well, and if there is one who took seriously the instruction to carry the Light to all nations, it was the apostle Paul. He was converted on the road to Damascus by a blinding Light and later completed three missionary journeys of heroic proportions. Antioch, Pamphylia, Phrygia, Galatia, Cyprus, Thessalonica, Athens, Corinth, Philippi, and Rome were some of the places Paul's journeys brought him. And in these places he did not always find universal welcome. In his second letter to the Corinthians he writes:

> *Five times I have received at the hands of the Jews the forty lashes less one. Three times I have been beaten with rods; once I was stoned. Three times I have been shipwrecked; a night and a day I have been adrift at sea; on frequent journeys, in danger from rivers, danger from robbers, danger from my own people, danger from Gentiles, danger in the city, danger in the wilderness, danger at sea, danger from false brethren; in toil and hardship, through many a sleepless night, in hunger and thirst, often without food, in cold and exposure. And, apart from other things, there is the daily pressure upon me of my anxiety for all the churches.* — 2 Corinthians 11:24-28

I have heard stories of lost luggage, missed connections, poor accommodations, hazardous driving conditions, and questionable cuisine from some who have taken the "Journeys of Paul" tour of the Mediterranean, but thank goodness, I have yet to hear of a trip which could match the real thing for difficulty. The shipwreck of Paul from Acts 27 is considered one of the finest accounts of shipwreck in ancient literature. But for now let us ask again the question: *How does the Light move?*

Ephesians indicates that Paul is a prisoner. He is locked up. His freedom of movement is restricted. How can the Light move, if the courier of the Light is in prison? He has received his instruction to take the Light to all nations, so how can this happen when he is in lock down? And why must this be so difficult? In biblical times it was thought that a man could stand but 39 lashes and live. Christ was thus scourged before his crucifixion. Paul was thus scourged five times, beaten with rods, stoned once, three times shipwrecked, and spent a night and a day adrift at sea. Also for Paul there was a mysterious physical malady, a thorn in the flesh in his words, "to keep me from being too elated by the abundance of revelations ..." (2 Corinthians 12:7). Some have suggested that this may have been epilepsy, malaria, or an eye affliction; the Bible does not specify. But the impression is clear this courier of the Light found no easy road.

No Easy Road

This has remained the case — the courier of the Light finds no easy road. Consider the monk, concerned over the practices of his sixteenth century Church; he wrote a list of concerns and nailed them to the door of the Wittenberg Castle Church. Under threat of excommunication and physical harm, he stood his ground, and from his protest came the Protest-ant side of the Christian Church. The courier of the Light found no easy road.

Or think of the young black minister in the southern United States in the early 1960s. A Ph.D. in Theology from Boston University had not won him admiration from all quarters. He had become a mouthpiece for Negro interests in the South, but now he found himself incarcerated in a Birmingham jail. How can the

Light move if its courier is in jail? This courier of the Light found no easy road.

So, the road is not cleared for those who carry the Light. The stewardship of grace is placed in the hands of those who are afflicted. And the promise of the Church depends on the transmission of Light through scratched and scarred lenses. Even so the Light is on the move; sometimes shining forth from cells or from behind iron curtains, being carried by those who limp or stumble or by those of halting speech. The apostle Paul writes of having prayed to God about his thorn of the flesh:

> *Three times I besought the Lord about this, that it should leave me; but he said to me, "My grace is sufficient for you, for my power is made perfect in weakness." I will all the more gladly boast of my weakness, that the power of Christ may rest upon me. For the sake of Christ, then, I am content with weaknesses, insults, hardships, persecutions, and calamities; for when I am weak, then I am strong.* — 2 Corinthians 12:8-10

As Paul suggests, when we are couriers of the Light, it is in our weakness that God is seen as strong. And when the Light moves slowly or not at all, it is what happens near the Light which brings glory to God. It is the power and beauty of the Light which draws others to it, and it is the strength of the Light which offers hope to those who need. For we are not the Light and we do not contain it. We are simply its good stewards for a time and are sent forth to share it as we are able.

What Happens Near The Light

In the nineteenth century, lighthouses on the U.S. coasts were tended by lighthouse keepers and their families. If a man who tended the light took ill or became disabled, often the work was picked up by his wife or children. Such was the case of Hosea Lewis. Having become, in 1853, the keeper of the light on Lime Rock Island at Newport, Rhode Island, Lewis suffered a stroke four years later, at which time his teenage daughter Ida assumed responsibility for the light. Each day included cleaning the reflectors, trimming the wick, and filling the oil reservoir at sunset and midnight, along with providing for her father's care. With long and demanding tasks, Ida was unable to continue her schooling, but daily delivered her siblings to class, whatever the weather, by rowing the 500 yards to the mainland. In the mid-1800s, it was unusual to see a woman maneuvering a boat, but Ida became well skilled and well known for handling the heavy craft.

The teenager gained a measure of fame at age sixteen when she rescued four young men after their boat capsized. She rowed to their aid, hearing their screams as they clung to their overturned craft. On March 29, 1869, Ida saved two drowning servicemen from nearby Fort Adams. Public knowledge of Ida's courage spread as far as Washington, inspiring President Ulysses S. Grant to visit Ida at Newport later that year. Ida rescued another two soldiers in 1881, for which she was awarded the U.S. Lifesaving Service's highest medal.

In early February of that year the two soldiers were crossing from Newport to Lime Rock Island on foot when the ice gave way. Ida, the lighthouse keeper, came running with a rope. Ignoring peril to herself from weak and rotten ice, she pulled one, then the other to safety. All told, Ida Lewis personally saved something like 25 people in fifty-plus years of keeping the light. Her last reported rescue came at age 63 when she saved a friend who had fallen into the water on her way to visit Ida on the island. "Asked where she found stength and courage for such a feat, Ida answered: 'I don't know, I ain't particularly strong. The Lord Almighty gives it to me when I need it, that's all.' " [1]

And when the Light moves not at all, it is what happens near the Light which brings glory to God. It is the power of the Light which offers hope to those who are in need. For we are not the Light and we do not contain it. We are simply its good stewards for a time.

Walking With The Light

When I was a boy, I made a big mistake. I attended summer camp as the youngest camper in my session. The first afternoon I noticed the assistant camp director, Tommy, was recovering from a broken ankle and in a walking cast. This for me was not a good week of camp. I was the slowest in the races, was the first to spill my tray at lunch, and when we told scary stories around the camp fire, I got scared — *really* scared. The other boys decided that I would be an easy target, and I started finding unappealing earthy things in my bunk, and not finding personal belongings which had been hidden.

Tommy realized there was a budding problem and began showing up, as if by a sixth sense, when I was about to receive a dose of creative mischief. Each night after lights out I would watch from my top bunk the path through the woods. Since my bunk had the best view of the path, my cabinmates said I was supposed to give the alert when a counselor was coming for bed check. Each night I watched and each night finally I saw the beam of a flashlight bobbing peculiarly in the woods. And each night I saw its bob, I knew it was Tommy limping up the path. He would enter and check each bunk, quietly speaking to each of the boys, saving my bunk for last, pausing a little longer at mine making sure to compliment me on some progress I was making on something or other. Every night I watched for the Light and every night it came.

I don't remember the names of my cabinmates nor do I remember much of what we learned at camp that year, but I do remember Tommy and the bobbing of the Light as he carried it. I could tell at a distance and even in the dark who was coming by the way he carried the Light.

I suppose that's the way it is as we limp through our lives, afflicted as we may be. God knows who is coming, because he knows how we carry the Light. The speed of Light for God is the speed at which we move as we carry it. One speed is not preferred over another, so much as is good journeying. For we are not the Light and we do not contain it. We are simply good stewards of the Light for a time and are sent forth to share it as we are able.

---

1. Mary Louise Clifford, "Keeper of the Light," *American History,* Sept/October 1996, p. 28.

Moving At The Speed Of Light:
At The Jordan

Acts 10:34-43

$Peter$ had long practiced a religion which required the separation of Jews and Gentiles, and following Christ's ascension Peter continued to be a practicing Jew. Through the example of Christ, Peter began to think differently about those who were considered ritually unclean and unacceptable to God. Earlier in Acts 10, Peter has been staying in Joppa in the home of one who practiced an "unclean" profession, Simon the Tanner.

From there he receives the call from God to travel to Ceasarea to the home of Cornelius the centurion, the "Italian Cohort," to preach to uncircumcised Gentiles which is where we find him in today's text. Peter's focus is shifting beyond Jerusalem. "Go into all the world and make disciples...." Peter and his companions baptize many Gentiles at the home of Cornelius and are persuaded to stay at Caesarea for some days. Peter preaches, "God shows no partiality, but in every nation any one who fears him and does what is right is acceptable to him" (Acts 10:34-35).

Many Are baptized ...

A little boy sits in the third row pew with his big sister; his feet won't touch the floor. It is hard sitting still in "big people worship," but his parents think it important today. Sister points to direct his attention. Mommy and Daddy stand in front with the minister as he sprinkles water on Baby Sister's head. Mommy wipes away a tear.

Confirmation day is near, but first Sally and a few others from her Confirmation class kneel before God's altar. The pastor pauses before each one, placing moistened hands on each head and praying the prayer, "I baptize you in the name of the Father, the Son, and the Holy Spirit. Amen." Sally feels the pastor's hands tremble as he prays.

A man comes to an usher before Sunday worship. Would the pastor be willing to baptize him today? "Come with me," the usher replies. The two arrive at the pastor's study a few minutes before worship is to begin. The pastor has not seen this man before. They chat briefly. The pastor explains baptism. "This church does not regularly baptize adults," the pastor warmly explains, "so this is a very special Sunday for us and for you." In a few minutes, the pastor baptizes the man and at the close of the service the church greets in friendliness the newly baptized fellow. They never hear from him again.

The family is gathered. Grandmother has been a familiar presence at several of the churches in town over the years, and though her parents never walked through the door of a church, including on their wedding day, she always made sure that her children got to Sunday School. Over the years they each have chosen a church, but not Grandmother — she always felt "kinda funny" that she'd never been baptized. So today she is in her nicest housecoat, her hair has been fixed, and there are fresh sheets on the bed. No one expects that Grandmother is at the end yet, but this latest illness has clearly taken something out of her. So everyone was pleased and a little relieved when she brought up the idea that "Maybe it is time to get the preacher over here to take care of something I probably should have done long ago." And "that woman minister" comes to the house, the one everyone is surprised they like, and baptizes Grandmother in the name of the Father, the Son, and the Holy Spirit.

The baby was born two months premature. He has a serious lung concern. Doctors are not predicting that he will live. "We just don't know," is all they will say. The mother, after a difficult labor, is now up to a ride in a wheelchair and asks to be wheeled to neonatal intensive care. The baby's parents, both clergy, and a family friend, also a minister, slip quietly into the baby area.

They do not believe that the baby's salvation is in danger with or without baptism, but respectfully they ask the nurse for a bowl of water. Then, only able to reach to the baby's foot through an opening in the incubator, they moisten his heel, baptizing in the name of the Father, and the Son, and the Holy Spirit.

At Cornelius' home in Ceasarea, many were baptized. Each Sunday many are baptized.

Jesus At The Jordan

Recently, two girls were seen by their mother "playing Bethlehem" with "Holy Family" stick figures they made in Sunday school, and a toy limousine. "What are you playing?" asks Mother. "Bethlehem," one responds. "This is baby Jesus; these are baby Jesus' mommy and daddy; and (lifting the modern motor vehicle) this is what the star from the east rides in."

Jesus rode no limo when he came to John the Baptist at the Jordan. He traveled from Nazareth to Jericho, probably with his family, a trip of four or five days on foot, to be baptized by John for the forgiveness of sins (a variation of the Jewish purification ritual). By then he had lived thirty years in Nazareth, a village influenced by the Essene sect of Judaism. He learned the trade of his earthly father, held a place of honor and responsibility among his siblings as the firstborn son, and assumed the role of head of the family at Joseph's death, though the biblical record does not indicate when this occurred. Following his temptation in the wilderness, it is likely that Jesus returned to John to assist in John's baptizing and gathering of disciples.

All the while his nation was an occupied state. Rome had installed local leadership which taxed the people heavily and engaged in glorious building projects. Jesus faithfully practiced the religion of his childhood and had seen the Jewish religious leaders try to stay on the right side of Rome while retaining the Temple's ritualistic tradition.

Preaching Peace

Peter claims in Acts 10 that Jesus preached peace. How did Jesus preach peace? Jesus lived in a time of conflict. The rights of people were not respected in any modern sense. (Occasionally in Paul's ministry his Roman citizenship earned him a different kind of treatment, but that was out of respect for the state not the individual.) A person thought to be at cross purposes with the state could be flogged, beaten, imprisoned, or crucified with little proof. It is told that 2,000 were killed in a mass crucifixion on one occasion simply to make a point. Part of the inertia which powered Christ into ministry was the beheading of John the Baptist, and Jesus knew that he, also, would come to a violent earthly end.

So what did he preach? Turn the other cheek, walk the second mile, those who live by the sword will die by the sword, blessed are the peace makers, let the children come.

Consider These Scenes

Jesus was setting out on his journey and a man came running and knelt before him. "Good Teacher," he asked, "what must I do to inherit eternal life?"

"You know the commandments," Jesus responded. " 'Do not kill; Do not commit adultery; Do not steal; Do not bear false witness; Do not defraud; Honor your father and mother.' "

And the man, still kneeling, said to him, "Teacher, all of these I have kept from my youth."

And Jesus, looking upon him, loved him, saying, "You lack one thing; go, sell what you have, and give to the poor, and you will have treasure in heaven; and come, follow me."

But the man became sad, for he had great possessions.

Jesus teaches: "Give to the poor," and "How hard it will be for those who have riches to enter the kingdom of God!" (Mark 10:17-23).

Hard it is when we are rich to enter the kingdom of God. Who is rich and who is poor?

Have you ever been rich and felt poor, or made your greatest achievement and not been able to celebrate? Or accomplished exactly what you set out to do and wondered if you had done the right thing?

Lee Atwater planned and executed George Bush's 1988 presidential victory. He grew up with two burning goals which he desired to achieve before age 35: to be Chairman of the Republican National Party and to manage a presidential campaign successfully. He did both.

Life magazine interviewed Mr. Atwater a short time before he died of brain cancer. Professionally he described himself as relentless, ruthless. After identifying an enemy's weakness, he attacked without mercy, made the enemy look comical — key strategies to which he was cruelly committed. He used Willie Horton against Dukakis on the crime issue and suggested that Bush's opponent, riding in a tank with that small odd helmet, "looked like a squirrel."

In the *Life* article, Atwater reminds us what the 1980s were about — acquiring wealth, prestige, and power. "I acquired more than most. But you can acquire all you want and still feel empty." Toward the end, Lee Atwater discovered something: "My illness helped me to see that what was missing in society is what was missing in me: a little heart and a lot of Brotherhood." [1]

Jesus teaches: "How hard it will be for those who have riches to enter the kingdom of God!"

Jesus was on his way to Jerusalem as he entered a village, where he was met by ten lepers standing at a distance. "Jesus, Master, have mercy on us," they cried out. And Jesus called back to them, "Go show yourselves to the priests," and as they went their way they were cleansed.

Then seeing that he was cleansed, one of them, a Samaritan, turned back praising God and falling at Jesus' feet, giving him thanks.

"Where are the nine? Were not ten cleansed?" Jesus asked. "Will no one return and give praise to God except this foreigner?" Then Jesus said to the Samaritan, "Rise and go your way; your faith has made you well" (Luke 17:11-19).

Jesus teaches thanksgiving to God, and heals those who are oppressed by the devil.

The Pharisees, seeking to test him, brought a woman to him who had been caught in adultery. "The law of Moses says we should stone such. What do you say about her?" Jesus paused, squatted down, and wrote with his finger in the dust. The agitated

Pharisees persisted. Jesus stood up. "Let him who is without sin among you cast the first stone." Jesus bent down once more, drawing in the dust again with his finger. *Thump . . . thump . . . thump* — the sound of heavy rocks falling harmlessly to earth. Leaving their rocks, the Pharisees went their way, beginning with the eldest, until Jesus was left alone with the woman standing before him on the road in the midst of the discarded rocks (John 8:3-11).

In ancient Israel stoning was the most common of capital punishments. Its most formal application was for the offender to be pushed off a ten-foot scaffold, and if he or she survived the fall, a witness to the crime would throw the first stone, followed by others. As stones are readily available throughout the region, sometimes stoning resembled more of a lynching. In any form, this was punishment up close and personal for the offender and for the ones casting the stones. It did not bring instantaneous death, but was painful, brutal, and required sustained effort. It made an impression on those casting the stones and on the community.

What was in the minds of the Pharisee/executioners as they brought the woman to Jesus ? Her crime would be used as a convenience to embarrass the teacher. Was their rage toward her offense fueled by their hatred toward him? As they dropped their stones and went their way, did their anger toward the teacher burn within them all the more?

And what was in the mind of this woman scared out of her wits? Had she resigned herself to her fate? How long did it take before she was calm enough to hear what Jesus was saying to her? As she stepped over the rocks to be on her way, did she sense that her life had been given back to her?

Jesus teaches: "Go and sin no more."

Jesus preaches peace with God to the baptized and to those who would be or could be baptized. He is the one who was twice baptized: once by John in the Jordan and again on Calvary when the ones who would have stoned the adulterous woman got another crack at him. He offers us the Kingdom of God on earth and treasure in heaven. But not all baptized Christians return to give thanks. It is hard to imagine how one could have his life given back to him and behave as if it is no big deal. It is hard to know how one could catch a glimpse of the Kingdom, and sadly be on his way because worldly wealth has become his god. It is hard to be up close and personal with the cross, hearing his groans and not feel the demand his second baptism places upon us. Jesus preaches peace with God to the baptized and to those who would or could be baptized. And we have the opportunity to return to him again and again. Sometimes we live as if we forget what he did and how he gave us back our lives.

But now as we set out to be on our way and step across the stones which could have been heaped on our heads, maybe we will hear the echo of his voice or remember how he stooped to draw in the dust, thinking of how he could advocate for us ... thinking of how to describe for us his love.

----

1. Lee Atwater with Todd Brewster, "The Last Campaign," *Life* magazine, XIV (February 1991), pp. 58-62.

Moving At The Speed Of Light:
In Corinth Or Cana?

1 Corinthians 1:1-9

It is hard to know what more can be said about marriage. Weddings are stressors. The planning, the showers, the many opinions, the money, the lists, the social pressures ... who can survive a wedding?

The summer before my teenage bride and I were wed in our September nuptials, we worked as lifeguards at a local swimming pool, making buckets of money. We were between our sophomore and junior years in college and had all the worldly possessions that one would expect from two who had partially furnished two dorm rooms. The other lifeguards at the pool threw a nice poolside picnic/party/shower for us at the end of the swimming season and the pool owner kicked in for the gift. We had great fun, including several gag gifts and my driving a tricycle (complete with tin cans attached and a "Just Married" sign) through an obstacle course with Beth as my passenger on the back.

The time came for opening *the gift,* a beautifully wrapped box about two and a half feet on a side. Tearing away the paper, Beth saw printed on the box the words "Home Made Ice Cream Freezer." One of the guards clarified, "That's not what it is. We just used the box." To which Beth responded, "Good thing, because that's just about the last thing we would ever need."

When the people of Nazareth took Jesus out to throw him off the cliff after he preached, I think it may have been because of his preaching, or it may have been because they gave him a gift and he did not think before he spoke while opening it. At any rate we *loved* our home made ice cream freezer our first year of marriage and used it often.

* * * * * * * * * *

The rural white frame church is filling for the wedding of a hometown girl. The pastor knows most everyone on the bride's side, but is less familiar with the family and friends of the groom. The prelude music is well along when it becomes clear that the church will be filled to overflowing. The resident village soloist is singing a lovely rendition of "O Promise Me" when a terrific clanging begins in Fellowship Hall, located directly behind the altar. A distressed, quizzical look comes over the soloist who continues to sing. She gives a quick "help me" glance to the young pastor, who immediately responds by heading toward the noise. Entering Fellowship Hall, he finds two ushers trying hastily to load forty folding chairs onto a metal cart. Quickly the pastor tries to slow them down, at first using overly dramatic sign language and then assuring, "It's okay, fellows. Take it easy. They won't start without us." At which time, one usher wheels around and grabs the preacher by his tie, pulling his face close, their noses almost touching.

"Now we'll see who's going to be quiet!" the usher says in a loud, raspy voice.

"I couldn't think what to do," the pastor later reported, "so I threw up my arms and said, 'The eleventh commandment is Thou shalt not punch the preacher.' "

Who Can Survive A Wedding?

Jesus and his budding group of disciples are invited to a wedding at Cana in Galilee. Jesus' family is also there. After a time, the wine runs out and Jesus' mother mentions this to him. This seems to irritate Jesus, or at least he doesn't appreciate being volunteered at this particular moment.

So Jesus instructs the servants, "Fill these jars with water," gesturing to the six stone jars used for the Jewish rite of purification. The servants quickly gather up everyone they can find to help carry the 150 gallons of water needed to fill the jars. The task completed, some "water" is drawn for the steward to taste. The steward informs the bridegroom, "Every man serves the good wine first;

66

and when men have drunk freely, then the poor wine; but you have kept the good wine until now" (John 2:1-11).

A more modern waiter might have said, "Ah, sir, we thought the hors d'oeuvres were the entrées and the guests have already eaten dessert. And ah ... well, we just discovered your two hundred wedding entrées still in the warmers, ah, do you want us to box 'em?" ... We can only imagine the surprise of the bridegroom.

Jesus did not want to be called on. What he asked of the servants was not easy. When it was all said and done, he did a great thing that may not have entirely worked out. Who can survive a wedding?

Collision At Corinth

Paul established a church in Corinth, a crossroads town on a narrow peninsula of Achaia. Corinth embodied considerable commercial vigor as a natural trading center between east and west, with industry developing based largely on slavery. The citizenry of Corinth consisted of Romans, Greeks, Orientals, and Jews from Egypt, Asia Minor, and Syria. Each of these groups imported its own customs and religious beliefs. In this conglomeration of beliefs and customs, speaking in tongues, ecstasy, and prophesy received attention and value. It was almost impossible to avoid eating meat which had been sacrificed to gods at funeral banquets or public festivals.

And while writing to encourage the saints at Corinth and to instruct them, Paul was also concerned about the values and lifestyles that these new Christians saw all around them in its pagan city. How would the values of the surrounding society affect the values of those within the church? Paul's key symbol in response is *the body*: the body of Jesus Christ, the church as the body of Christ, and the individual's body. "Paul's concern with the body expresses his concern with the religious boundaries between the Christian community and its pagan society."[1] So there was a collision at Corinth within the church and within the family similar to the collision we face within the church and the family in our time.

How will we maintain our sense of balance? When is it okay to compromise? What is the role of man/husband/father and woman/wife/mother?

Paul claims: "You are not lacking in any spiritual gift, as you wait for the revealing of our Lord Jesus Christ ..." but waiting for the Lord seems long, and waiting for the revealing of his wisdom in these matters seems long as well. There is a collision in Corinth, and we need a wisdom beyond our own.

When The Wine Runs Out

I wonder if, after he turned the water from the six stone jars into wine, Jesus said, "And no refills." At the wedding feast the wine ran out. Jesus created some more. Presumably the partyers drank this new better wine and then it ran out. This is a fact of life in marriage. It may take a while. It may take a good long while, but it happens.

For a while, the energy of the new relationship carries us, but then if something more is not there, the wine runs out and the party's over. Oddly enough, signs that the wine will run dry begin in many relationships with the wedding and possibly with planning the wedding. Free and easy lives begin to give way to the responsibilities and roles of wife and husband. If what "I" want is paramount, then the dry wine jar begins to show up early.[2]

Consider this spouse's desires: *I* need someone who is a great bread winner. *I* need someone who provides a wonderful home, who keeps *me* in stylish clothes, and *my* children in the best schools. *I* don't want a spouse who travels or comes home late from the office or who is stressed at the end of the day. *I* want *my* spouse to be a civic leader and a pillar of the church. And *I* want my spouse to exercise regularly and *I* want my spouse to control "over-exposure to the sun" so that *my* spouse will always look young.

Lately we have been learning that building a good marriage calls for the claiming of a shared marital vision — what is our dream for our marriage; what do we want our lives together to be? If I take my *I* out of the limelight, can our relationship create a *we* which is solid and lasting? In 1864 E.W. Buser went off to war. Too young to fight, he served as a drummer, helping the troops

68

travel by keeping cadence. While in Tennessee he carved the center out of a uniform button, which was much larger and thicker than a modern button. On the edge of the button he inlayed silver, gold, and mother of pearl depicting clasping hands, a woman's hand in a man's. So skilled was he as an artisan that on the left ring finger of one of the hands can be seen a wedding band. He sent the ring home to his sweetheart with a proposal for marriage. Out of the materials of war, came a beautiful symbol of love and the sign of two individuals committing to find the *we*.

When You Find The Best Wine — Sip It

Hugh and Gayle Prather claim that "there is simply no mistake to be made in choosing a mate or at least the chances are very small that you will choose someone who is truly dangerous. You *will* wind up with someone with far more flaws that you originally thought."[3] Choosing a mate is like selecting a bottle of wine with no label — no tasting, no sniffing, no opening. You may admire the bottle and even consider the richness of the color, but that's it. And by the way this is your last bottle for a lifetime — make it last ... So you want to know how much it costs?

The Prathers go on to point to the possibility that *any two people could love each other.* In some cultures marriages are arranged, and sometimes deep affection grows despite the prescribed nature of a relationship's beginning. The Prathers go on to claim that their counseling has shown them that the strengths and weaknesses of marriage partners almost invariably complement each other. "However negative a couple thought were the reasons that brought them together, it is usually clear that a part of their mind knew what it was doing. It's as if God sent you a box of your missing parts."[4]

As we have seen above, there are many threats to a good marriage in Corinth, and we all in some ways live there. The demands and values of the community, the work place, social circles, previous involvements, the complex challenges of raising children, all can threaten a strong, life-enhancing marriage. In Corinth, it is the *I* that counts, and this *I* can become the instrument of dissection to the *we*.

Does this mean that we have to give up the hope of having joy and satisfaction in the marital bond? Must we so subjugate our desires, appetites, interests, and dreams that they become functionally nonexistent? Maybe yes and maybe no.

Learn where the best wine is to be found, and when you find the best wine, sip it.

Rick was a young man showing some musical promise. He had a creative sensitivity far advanced among his peers. He was pleasant, cooperative, and a good team player. His encouraging half smile and subtle humor had a way of making you just feel good. This is why the community was rocked when at the end of middle school Rick was discovered to have a kind of cancer which is difficult to treat.

"Often it can be sent into remission, sometimes for long periods, but it almost always comes back," the doctors told his parents. "We are making advances all the time in this. We will take it a day at a time, say our prayers, and hope for the best."

Liz had known Rick since elementary school, and because of their interest in music, the two had become friends . She was hard hit by the discovery of Rick's illness, but she held her fears at bay so their relationship mostly continued in a normal way.

Each time Rick's illness flared, the unpleasant treatments were able to send it into remission. Through it all Rick's spirits remained surprisingly balanced. In his sophomore year, Rick asked Liz to the spring dance and from that time, they went out often and called each other "my best date." Rick's illness continued to be a problem from time to time, and they weathered his illness together, Liz supporting Rick.

High school commencement came and went, and both continued their education at a local junior college while working part-time jobs. This was when Liz came to my office. Obviously nervous, she confided that she had asked Rick to marry her. The two sets of parents were supportive and would help with living expenses. I gently asked if there was a pregnancy involved, to which Liz responded, "Oh no, Rick can't have children ... because of the treatments." We talked about the possibilities for their future together and the responsibilities of marriage, most of which given what the couple had been through, Liz already had grasped.

So we had a beautiful wedding, and as I read Paul's words I understood them differently than before: "Love is patient and kind, love is not jealous or boastful, it is not arrogant or rude. Love does not insist on its own way ... Love bears all things, believes all things, hopes all things, endures all things...."

In the coming months we saw these two have the uncanny ability to find the best wine — time to share music, time to share with family and friends, with God — and sip it. They continued as they could to go about their ordinary activities, and when the hard times came, they shared those with us and with God also. And in so doing they found the best wine even in times of calamity and sadness.

As it turned out we couldn't hold Rick for long. Liz and Rick were married for only a year-and-a-half before the illness took him. We had a service of celebration with lots of music, some of which Rick had written. We played a tape on which we heard Rick sing. Liz seemed sad, but okay, even quietly satisfied that they had chosen to make this journey in this way, and seemed to know that in a little while another chapter of life would need to be written.

As we lingered in the cemetery on that crystal blue clear day, my eyes were cast again on Rick's young widow and Paul's words came to mind: "Love bears all things, believes all things, hopes all things, endures all things ... Love never ends...."

The Road From Corinth To Cana

Paul says in his letter to the Corinthian Christians that we are not lacking in any spiritual gift, as we wait for the revealing of our Lord Jesus Christ, which is to say that we in our marriages and in our families are equipped to travel the road from Corinth to Cana. We are constantly threatened by the voices and values which would distract us, detain us, degrade us, and disorient us. But we have the ability to travel a road which leads away from those voices, and as we travel, those voices which would claim and destroy us will become fading and faint. But still it is a demanding and dangerous road, and the time of trouble will come. So as beautiful as

71

is the symbol of the engagement ring with two hands clasping, I think the artisan had it wrong. For the symbol for the marital *we* should not be hands joined as if holding or shaking hands, instead travelers on the marital road form the *we* by grasping each other's wrists (hand to wrist and hand to wrist), a grip used in lifesaving to form the human chain. For the stormy waters of life will come with surprising force threatening to sweep us away, but partners in good marriages know how to hold on.

So who can survive a wedding? We all can, but *surviving marriage* is a challenge, especially if we hope to find Cana and the best wine, along the way.

---

1. Elizabeth Schussler Fiorenza, "1 Corinthians," *Harpers Bible Commentary* (San Francisco: Harper, 1988), p.1169.

2. Judith S. Wallerstein and Sandra Blakeslee, *The Good Marriage* (New York: Warner Books,1995), p. 62.

3. Hugh and Gayle Prather, *I Will Never Leave You* (New York: Bantam, 1995), p. 62.

4. *Ibid.*, pp. 63-64.

Moving At The Speed Of Light:
Nazareth: Family Ties

1 Corinthians 1:10-18

When I was a child and my mother started thinking out loud about "going home," she meant driving to Grandma's house a thousand miles away. This trip from Ohio to Nebraska with two parents, five children, and sometimes a dog did not happen in our unairconditioned family sedan without considerable planning and effort. Just packing the car strained family cordiality and tested my father's training as an engineer. His plan was always the same: Be on the road shortly after midnight and drive all night so that the younger children would sleep through the first several hundred miles. Sometimes we would stop for sightseeing at such places as Lincoln's Tomb in Springfield, Illinois, or to admire the St. Louis Gateway Arch. Always we were struck with awe as we crossed the "big bridge" over the mighty Mississippi.

My favorite places were the diners and pancake houses where we took our meals. Sometimes we did not drive "straight through"; instead we stayed a night in a motel, one with a pool if we were lucky. Sleeping arrangements were always tenuous: who gets the beds, the roll away, and the floor? I didn't mind the floor, but the snoring chorus which would erupt without warning left this light sleeper pacing, pushing toilet tissue into his ears, and once attempting to sleep in the bath tub.

It was difficult to manage the pet over such a long trip. The year we took Fritz, our dachshund, we had our windows fully rolled down as we approached St. Louis, creating quite a breeze at seventy miles per hour. Why Fritz decided to jump at that particular moment I will never know, but he was one lucky dachshund that my sister had a good hold on his leash. I remember my father's frantic turn onto the berm, slowing the car, all the while my sister holding little Fritz by the leash, dangling outside the car above the speeding pavement until we stopped ... That dog always seemed a little longer to me after hanging out there like that.

And we always made it to the little town where my mother grew up. We always found a warm welcome; always good food, clean beds, good conversation, and many games of checkers. These were very pleasant times almost entirely except for the visits of a few in town who never seemed to understand how or why my mother could have moved so far away. They hoped someday she would come back to stay and implied strongly that somehow the world would have been a better place had my mother always remained a hometown girl. These discussions were painfully repetitive. They never seemed to go anywhere and they always made my mother uncomfortable.

Where Was Jesus' Home?

So far as we know, Jesus lived most of his life, thirty years or so, in Nazareth. Though settled early, the town had been abandoned for hundreds of years because of the exile to Babylon and resettled by a clan "of the davidic line" around 100 B.C. In Jesus' time the size of the clan-settlement Nazareth was 120 to 150 people. In other words, it was a small village, where Jesus lived surrounded by his extended family.

Did Jesus Have Strained Family Ties?

Though we know during his ministry Jesus' family ties became strained, this clearly was not always the case. Jesus traveled with his family to the wedding at Cana of Galilee and "after this (the wedding) he went down to Caper'naum with his mother and his brothers and his disciples. There they stayed for a few days" (John 2:12). A family group also likely accompanied him when he went to be baptized by John, his cousin, in the Jordan.

But strained family ties did develop as Jesus began to locate his ministry more and more in Capernaum. One can only imagine how the hopes of Nazareth were placed on Jesus. The residents, who almost all were related to him, had seen him grow in wisdom and stature, until there was a sense of great expectancy. Jesus' family was of the davidic line, the line from which the prophets said the messiah would come. And just when he seemed to be coming to full flower, he went to live with some fishermen by the lake.

Jesus' Other Home

Jesus in fact did make Capernaum his home and through his ministry, as much as Jesus had one, he made his home with Peter. So imagine how his family felt when they showed up at Peter's house while Jesus was teaching, having made the trip from Nazareth — Jesus' mother, brothers, and sisters.

Some think they had come to bring him back to his real home — Nazareth. They were concerned about him. They knew how the crowds were pressing upon him and that sometimes he was forgetting to eat. People were saying, "He is beside himself; he is out of his mind!" (Mark 3:21). And there had been controversy with the Pharisees!

So here in public, with a crowd seated about him, Jesus was told, "Your mother and your brothers are outside, asking for you."

And Jesus asked, "Who are my mother and my brothers?" Then looking at the crowd seated about him he said, "Here are my mother and my brothers! Whoever does the will of God is my brother, and sister, and mother" (Mark 3:32-35). What a welcome! Imagine how his family felt.

So when he did return home to his kin in Nazareth and attended a synagogue service, a mixture of feelings about this young rabbi welcomed him. At first things went reasonably well. The service on that particular Sabbath was composed of the usual prayers and two readings. Jesus stood up to read and the scroll of the prophet Isaiah was handed to him:

"The Spirit of the Lord is upon me," he read, "because he has anointed me to preach good news to the poor. He has sent me to proclaim release to the captives and recovering of sight to the blind, to set at liberty those who are oppressed, to proclaim the acceptable year of the Lord" (Luke 4:18-19).

What hopeful words from the prophet Isaiah and how pleasantly they fell on the ears of Jesus' kin. And then he said, "Today this scripture has been fulfilled in your hearing." And the townspeople spoke well of him and were astonished at the gracious words spoken by this son of Joseph the carpenter.

But then things began to turn. Jesus continued, "Doubtless you will quote to me this proverb, 'Physician, heal yourself ...' " and the discussion took up Caper'naum and the desire of the people of Nazareth for Jesus to do at least as much for his clan in Nazareth as he has done for that *other* place.

And Jesus continued, his words to family, friends, and townspeople no longer gracious:

> *Truly, I say to you, no prophet is acceptable in his own country. But in truth, I tell you, there were many widows in Israel in the days of Eli'jah, when the heaven was shut up three years and six months, when there came a great famine over all the land; and Eli'jah was sent to none of them but only to Zar'ephath, in the land of Sidon, to a woman who was a widow. And there were many lepers in Israel in the time of the prophet Eli'sha; and none of them was cleansed, but only Na'aman the Syrian.*

By this time the faithful in the Nazareth synagogue had had just about enough of this upstart prophet who insisted on living elsewhere and thought he was too good for his own people. Their anger erupted into a small riot driving Jesus through town until they would have thrown him over a cliff ... but I suppose a dispute emerged among these angry relatives, maybe Jesus' brothers came to his defense. Somehow in the confusion Jesus walked right through the mob and went his way — back to Caper'naum[1] (Luke 4:21-30).

And when tempers had cooled in Nazareth they talked about the things Jesus had said to them and of how he bewildered them. "How could he have moved away?" They hoped sometime he would come back to stay. On one thing they could all agree: "The world would have been a better place had Jesus remained a hometown boy."

76

It appears that the tensions in Jesus' family centered around loyalty to Nazareth, the town of his upbringing, to his clan, and to his immediate family. After all, this was a family/clan/tribe which was of the davidic line from which the prophets said the next great king would come. "Jesus, don't forget the way home."

Likewise, the apostle Paul is concerned about divisions in the church at Corinth being caused by confused loyalty. So he writes an appeal for agreement and unity. Paul has heard that there is quarreling among the brethren and that some are saying, "I belong to Paul," or "I belong to Apol'los," or "I belong to Cephas," or "I belong to Christ." "Is Christ divided?" asks Paul (1 Corinthians 1:10-13).

In the Corinthian church there was a controversy over allegiance. To whom will we be loyal; to whom will we pledge our energy, our creativity, our wealth, our love, our lives? There are always many to whom we could give our allegiance and there are always many voices trying to persuade us that they are worthy of our trust and loyalty. Paul helped the Corinthian Christians to refocus on Christ. A good lesson for us all.

The tension in Jesus' family came because, after the synagogue education system of Nazareth had done a good job of bringing Jesus up in the faith, his family and friends wanted to dictate to him how he would practice his faith — which is always dangerous. How can one know how God will choose powerfully to use one of our loved ones? They wanted him to stay in Nazareth! If he had, where would that leave us? Sometimes God calls us forth to do the difficult or the seemingly unwise, but who are we to discourage another when one has heard a call of God? Focus on Christ! And belong to him, says Paul.

Clergyman/songwriter Benjamin Hanby wrote the children's Christmas song, "Up On The Housetop"; the hymn, "Who Is He In Yonder Stall?"; and "Darling Nelly Gray," the pre-Civil War ballad which swept the nation advancing anti-slavery values. He was called the "Uncle Tom's Cabin" of song.

And it is not surprising that Ben would turn his attention to anti-slavery concerns, because his father, William Hanby, was a leader in the Underground Railroad. In 1850 the Fugitive Slave

Law was passed, making it easier for Southern slave owners to recover runaway slaves. William Hanby hid slaves in his barn. Ben often helped with their food or secretly escorted them to wagons which would take them to the next stop north on the Underground Railroad.

William Hanby was an outspoken critic of the Fugitive Slave Law, heaping ridicule on a law that would make it a felony to feed a starving slave. William Hanby was ready when asked how he could knowingly break this law. He replied:

> ... when a law keeps a people from humanity, it is no longer the voice of God; it is a counterfeit and must not be obeyed. When a manmade law is in conflict with God's law, there is no compromise....[2]

And he would quote Saint Peter: "We ought to obey God rather than men" (Acts 5:29).

William Hanby was a vigorous critic of the Fugitive Slave Law and well he should have been. William was the child of an indentured servant, and his mother had William bound over for service after her husband died and she could no longer take care of her five young children. He received brutal treatment, and his master required him to lie and cheat in business, so William escaped. He later described his flight:

> ... on the night of Wednesday the 24th of March, 1828, about 12 o'clock at night I bade farewell to Beallsville and bent my course towards the beautiful state of Ohio. No one can describe the anguish of my heart that night and for the days afterwards. Leaving a poor and dependent mother behind, very poorly clad, my spirits crushed by the treatment I had received, and every moment dreading the footsteps of my hated master in pursuit of me, who had already declared repeatedly that he would follow me to Hell if I ever attempted to run away.[3]

William Hanby was a vigorous critic of the Fugitive Slave Law and well he should have been, because he hated what the law was doing to some of God's children, and he knew their pain and fear and suffering. So he knew where his loyalty belonged; he knew to whom he would give his allegiance. "Choose this day whom you will serve ... but as for me and my house, we will serve the LORD." Joshua 24:15 was a foundation of William Hanby's life.

Paul heard that there was quarreling among the brethren and wrote an appeal for agreement and unity. In the Corinthian church there was a controversy over allegiance. To whom will we be loyal; to whom will we pledge our energy, our creativity, our wealth, our love, our lives? Paul helped the Corinthian Christians to refocus on Christ.

The family of Jesus helped him to learn and grow in the faith but then wanted to tell him how to live his faith and where to place his allegiance. It was hard for them to let him go; they could see the many challenges he would face, and sometimes they did not understand him or his mission. Certainly they were not early followers of Jesus, but in the end they did come around and *chose who they would serve.* For in the book of Acts, Jesus' family is seen as very much a part of the fellowship of believers, and Jesus' brother James oversees the church in Jerusalem.

> *Jesus said, "Greater love has no man than this, that a man lay down his life for his friends."* — John 15:13

> *James, brother of our Lord,*
> *saw this love in Jesus*
> *and later circa 62 AD.*
> *Jesus saw this love in James,*
> *when James was stoned*
> *by priestly authorities,*
> *and laid down his life,*
> *for the love of God,*
> *for the love of Christ,*
> *for the love of his brother,*
> Jesus.

_____

1. For an interesting treatment of Jesus' relationship with his family, see Bargil Pixner, *With Jesus Through Galilee According to the Fifth Gospel* (Israel: Corazin, 1992), pp. 49 ff.

2. Dacie Custer Shoemaker, *Choose You This Day: The Legacy of the Hanbys* (Westerville, OH: The Westerville Historical Society, 1983), p. 28.

3. William Hanby, "Autobiography" (Library, The Ohio Historical Society). Manuscript in the handwriting of William Hanby concerning his early life, religious experiences and travels up to 1857. Originally written at the request of John Lawrence, editor of *Unity Magazine*.

Moving At The Speed Of Light:
Jerusalem: What Word Would You Say?

1 Corinthians 1:18-31

"For the word of the cross is folly to those who are perishing," asserts Paul in First Corinthians. "But to us who are being saved, it is the power of God." The word of the cross ... folly to those who are perishing. To those who are being saved by it — to us — it is the Power of God. Imagine, if you will, the scene in Jerusalem: devout Jews gathered from every nation under heaven. There is a sound of mighty wind, tongues of fire light upon each of the disciples, who begin to speak as the Spirit gives them utterance. At the sound the multitude comes together, and they are bewildered because each one hears them speaking in his own language. "These are Galileans! How is it we understand?" (Acts 2:5-13).

When a word is spoken, it is accomplishment enough to understand when the word comes in our own language. We are told that most Americans use about 400 words of the English language about eighty percent of the time. Which is to say that the remaining 400,000 words to be found in the standard English language dictionary remain mostly unused. Carolyn Davidson helps us make our point with this short quiz. (Quiz answers may be found in footnotes.)

1) Tolerate the batologist!
a) a baseball team's incompetent batting instructor
b) a person who repeats without necessity the same thing
c) a bramble studying scientist.

2) Whoosh, a williwaw.
a) a ride on a Ferris wheel
b) a turn of the century Appalachian folk dance
c) a surprise, powerful gust of cold air.

3) No one needs a criticaster.
a) a large stick used by veterinarians to move zoo animals
b) the plant from which castor oil is made
c) an ineffective or inexperienced critic.

4) I've read about the splacknuc.
a) a tool used to apply mortar to bricks
b) a device used to attach climbers to the face of a mountain
c) Jonathan Swift mentions this unusual animal in *Gulliver's Travels*.

5) What a big herfuffle!
a) the shoulder harness used on a draft horse
b) a fuss, commotion
c) a woman's headdress or hat usually with feathers.

6) osculate —Romeo said to Juliet, "Let's osculate."
a) skip rope
b) dance using repeating oscillating motion
c) kiss.[1]

If you were among the disciples in Jerusalem that day, what Word would you say to those who had come from every nation under heaven? "For the word of the Cross is folly to those who are perishing; to us who are being saved, it is the Power of God." To speak a word and to be understood in our own language is accomplishment enough, but to speak a word which is known by those who come from afar is astonishing. "Parthians and Medes and Elamites and residents of Mesopotamia, Judea and Cappadocia, Pontus and Asia, Phrygia and Pamphylia, Egypt and the parts of Libya belonging to Cyrene, and visitors from Rome," those who come from the land of wisdom and those from the hallways of earthly power. Paul continues: "For it is written, I will destroy the wisdom of the wise, the cleverness of the clever I will thwart." So to those who come from afar, what would you say?

Omni magazine asks the question: "If an alien landed in your backyard, what would you say?" The question was asked to the governors of our fifty states, to the U.S. President and Vice President, to business leaders and luminaries in various fields of endeavor. A research vice president at AT&T Bell Labs responded, "Hopefully, [their advanced intelligence] would give them enough insight to avoid triggering a social calamity when one of them gets on a talk show...." George Carlin the comedian, answered: "Get out! Save yourselves! You don't know what you're getting into. Prolonged contact with our species can only degrade your present standards, whatever they are." Brereton C. Jones, Kentucky governor, said, "I would want to give them two items ... The U.S. Constitution and a copy of the Bible. The Constitution is the compilation of rules that we as a people have chosen to follow. The Bible ... is the compilation of rules that our Creator has chosen for us to follow. I would explain that we do not always abide by all of these, but we are striving to do so, and that is our ultimate goal."[2] If you were one of the disciples in Jerusalem on that day of rushing wind and tongues of fire, speaking to those who came from afar, what Word would you say?

Our words change with time, sometimes suddenly. Back in the summer of '97 when NASA landed a mission on Mars, how quickly did the meaning of *sojourner*, *Sagen Memorial Station*, *Barnacle Bill*, and *Yogi* change. "For consider your call, brethren; not many of you were wise according to worldly standards, not many were powerful, not many were of noble birth; but God chose what is foolish in the world to shame the wise, God chose what is weak in the world to shame the strong."

The devout Jews had gathered in Jerusalem from every nation under heaven. So what would you say to them in that time long ago — of God, of Jesus, of the church? What will you say to them now?

William Willimon in his book *Resident Aliens* suggests that we in the church live as a colony within an alien culture. In part the mission is to sustain and to protect the values, knowledge, and traditions which are uniquely ours as Christian men and women. We live in the midst of a culture which would overcome and consume us, trivialize us, tame and trample us, and yet we not only protect and defend our faith and traditions, we launch out from this place to bring the precious Word which has been entrusted to us.[3] So what Word will you say? And how will you say it? Some will be inclined to defer. "I need several more months of Bible Study; I think I will wait until I've read the latest book by Rabbi Kushner or Leo Buscaglia or Billy Graham's autobiography."

But there isn't time. The one who has come from afar is *in your backyard* or very nearby. What Word will you bring? Some will say, "I want them to know that I am a Christian and who is my master by the way that I live. My actions speak for me." Recently I was chatting with a friend about a man we both know. It surprised us to realize that we had both been a part of Alfred's life for some time. My friend had known Alfred for nearly two decades while I had known Al for a mere six years. "Well, the Al you know is not the same person he was twenty years ago. Then he was harsh and crude, quick to judge, a real terror. But lately something has changed. He seems kinder, more compassionate; he thinks of others more than himself." What I know and my friend doesn't know is that the change in Al is due to more than the process of aging and that within the last five or six years Al's life in the colony — the "church" colony — has taken on new importance and meaning. With secret pride, I am filled with thanks that God is doing something important in Alfred's life. But it is a tempered joy because to his friends and close business associates, Alfred has yet to reveal to whom the glory belongs.

So when you launch out, what Word will you say? And how will you say it? You don't have to be an expert in biblical archeology or ancient languages. You don't have time to read more books before you begin or to attend more classes. The time is now. What Word will you say and how will you say it?

Charles Kuralt, one of America's fine journalists, didn't *cover* the news. He said he stepped out of the way, never covering, blanketing, or obscuring the story with himself. A professor of journalism at the time of Kuralt's death wrote, "His preferred beat was America's heartland. Kuralt saw the special people all around us, and he told their stories in a way that journalism rarely takes the time to do.

"Some people have said that Kuralt likely wouldn't be hired for an on camera reporting job in today's news environment. Overweight, rumpled, and balding, he was the antithesis of modern broadcast news. Still, he was a news storyteller I could hold up as a model for my students."[4] What Word will you bring; what story will you tell?

Near my childhood home when it rained hard, a drainage ditch always turned into a raging torrent. All of the children in the neighborhood were instructed by frightened parents to stay away . One day when it was running fast, I sneaked away to play with my trucks near the torrent's edge. A great erosion had occurred, revealing a sloping mud bank. To retrieve a truck which had fallen to the edge of the water, I got out my black rubber snow boots. Stepping carefully into the mud, I quickly sank several inches. Frightened and stuck in the mud, I pulled my feet out of the boots sliding back up onto the top of the bank. Back to the house I went returning with my brother's snow boots — same result. Stuck in the mud. I had the same misfortune with my other brother's and *my father's* snow boots: four sets of boots stuck in the mud, where I shouldn't have been to begin with. I rehearsed the story I would tell my father upon his return home from work. What story would I tell and how would I tell it? I constructed and reconstructed, asked for editorial advice, prayed for Divine revelation. Finally, I told the story.

In sensitive times we think about how we will tell the story. Recently a pastor was visiting a parishioner in a hospital waiting room. He sat down next to her and as she spoke, her words caught. "The news about Mother is not good," she said, gathering herself. "I'll be better in a minute. The doctor was just here. It's hard saying it for the first time."

How will we tell the children; how will we tell our employer; what will we say to the neighbors?

In sensitive times we plan how we will tell the story. Likewise, let us plan how we will share the Greatest Story: that we have been visited by Someone sent here, that he assumed human form, the Word incarnate, and lived for 33 years. After his arrest, he was executed, but death's power was broken by God and he was raised to life. He met with his disciples after his resurrection and left them with a message for everyone on this planet. "I love you. That is why I died. Go now and tell the story." We need not be biblical archeologists, theologians, journalists, or entertainers. Simply speak the Word and to those who by the Word are being saved, it will be the Power of God.

Some might be asking, "Why is this so hard for me?" Because the story is precious, because its meaning for us is *life,* because our telling of it can never add to its glory — and that's the beauty of it. In its telling, we never cover, blanket, or obscure the Story. Instead we simply set it free to let it work as it will in our own lives and in the lives of those who hear. So, tell the Story as you see it unfolding in the special people all around us. Unfolding even in ourselves and we will be amazed — they will hear and understand.

---

1. Carolyn Davidson, *WORD-A-HOLIC QUIZ BOOK,* www.intex.net/faxes/awfta.htm
   Quiz answers: 1: b, 2: c, 3: c, 4: c, 5: b, 6: c.

2. David Sisler, "What Would You Say to an Alien?" *The Augusta Chronicle*, March 4,1995.

3. Stanley Hauerwas and William H.Willimon, *Resident Aliens* (Nashville: Abingdon Press, 1989).

4. John Weispfenning, "Kuralt Was Model of Good Journalism," *The Columbus Dispatch*, July 11, 1997, p. 11 A.

Moving At The Speed Of Light:
Athens: Unknown Apostles

1 Corinthians 2:1-12 (13-16)

How many people are helpful to us in a given stretch of time? How many are helpful to *you* in a given stretch of time? Folks whose names you may not know who go out of their way to help you out.

A while back a mother was driving home, and an eruption of discontent came from the back seat — two little boys who could not get along. She pulled off to the side of the road and stopped. Sensing there might be a mechanical failure, a police cruiser with two officers pulled up next to her inquiring if she needed help. "Well, you see, officer," she said, "I had such a commotion in the back seat that I knew it wouldn't be safe for me to continue driving." Picking up on the cue, the kindly officer glanced at the boys, at which time the four-year-old said, "Oh, we're sorry, officer. We'll never do it again. Please don't put us in jail!" Not surprisingly, things the next few weeks were calmer in the back seat.

How many folks whose names we may not know help us? How many whose names we know not, whose names will never be recorded in any gospel or in any book of history, have served God faithfully?

My wife and I were students at Bowling Green. We traveled home to Columbus through Bluffton, Ohio, with regularity. Late one Friday afternoon as we drove our older model car through Bluffton, steam started pouring from under the hood. We rattled into a filling station and stalled. I used all of my mechanical ability and did the only thing I could think of —got out of the car and threw open the hood. Shortly a mechanic joined me rubbing grease from his hands with a rag. Looking at the cloud of steam, I said confidently, "I think there's a problem with that propeller thing on the front of the motor."

"Does it fly?" he asked. "That propeller thing is attached to your water pump and you're going to need a new one."

I was nearly out of cash and without a credit card, I explained. "I guess I'll need to have somebody come up from Columbus to pick us up."

"Comin' back through here anytime soon?" he asked.

"Day after tomorrow," I responded.

"Hop in my truck!" he pointed. So Beth and I and the grease-covered mechanic hopped in his truck, making a fast trip to the auto parts store at a nearby town which was nearly closed for the day. He purchased a rebuilt water pump out of his own pocket and installed it for us, sending us on our way with only a handshake and a promise to pay when we returned.

How many have blessed us, trusted us, helped us on our way whose names we know not? Even in Jesus' circle we have unknown followers. Who were *the seventy* Jesus sent into mission two by two in the tenth chapter of Luke? In some cases we have names but little else: Simon, who is called Peter, and Andrew his brother, James the son of Zebedee and John his brother; Philip and Bartholomew, Thomas and Matthew the tax collector, and James, son of Alphaeus, and Thaddeus, Simon the Canaanean and Judas Iscariot who betrayed him. In Acts Peter is the dominant leader of the church in the early chapters and while undoubtedly "the twelve" were active and faithful, only three of them are mentioned as leaders in the entire book. Unknown disciples, unknown apostles?

Or what about Jesus' siblings? How many brothers did Jesus have? How many of them had the same name as one of his disciples? Jesus had four brothers and they are named James, Joseph, Judas, and Simon. And how many sisters? This we don't know, but by Gospel account there were "sisters" to Jesus. Unknown sisters, unknown apostles, unknown disciples? "What no eye has seen, nor ear heard, nor the heart of man conceived, what God has prepared for those who love him" (Paul's paraphrase of Isaiah 64:4).

When I was a child and learning to swim, I knew that I needed to swim a certain distance before I would be allowed to go into the deep end. So I set out from the shallow end to swim the length of the pool. As I was getting about two thirds of the way, I began to choke, began to be frightened and fatigued, began to cough and sputter. Before my fear turned to panic, there was a splash next to me in the water, an arm around my chest, a fast pulling motion and a voice saying, "Here, hold on to this," and I found myself safely at the side of the pool, grasping the pool gutter. An unknown life saver watching from above had leaped to my aid, deposited me safely at the side, and crawled out of the pool before I ever saw his face. And then he was back on the job. I know not his name, remember not his face, but I remember that he saved me.

And for a length of time Paul was an unknown apostle to the Jerusalem disciples. We remember how he met Jesus. He was on his way of persecution. Paul was present at the stoning of Stephen and had gone to the trouble of getting written authorization to persecute the Christians of Damascus. Paul, at that time called Saul, was on his way to Damascus when a blinding light drove him to his knees. And from that light came a voice, "Saul, Saul why do you persecute me?"

"Who are you, Lord?" asked Saul.

"I am Jesus, whom you are persecuting," said the voice. "But rise and enter the city and you will be told what you are to do."

And Paul arose from the ground and his eyes were open but he could see nothing. So they brought him to Damascus and after a time by God's power and by the courage of a believer named Anani'as, his sight was restored. After a while there in Damascus, he preached powerfully and proved to many that Jesus Christ is the Messiah, and the Jews began to plot against him. Paul had a narrow escape from Damascus, he was sneaked out of town by believers, and then went to Jerusalem where he attempted to join the disciples. But they were all afraid of him for they did not believe that he was a disciple. Who is this Paul? Is he not the man who made havoc among believers, attempting to bring them bound before the chief priests? An unknown to the Jerusalem disciples,

Paul was the unknown apostle. "To whom does his loyalty belong?" they wondered.

From here, we know Paul's story. He became known to them and he undertook three couragous/herculean missionary journeys. He established churches and encouraged believers. He wrote letters and instructed on theology and the practice of Christian living. And on one of his journeys he traveled to Athens. Entering the city he saw the altars and objects of worship used by the Athenians to appease their various gods. When he reached the place of public address, he preached,

> *Men of Athens, I perceive that in every way you are very religious. For as I passed along, and observed the objects of your worship, I found also an altar with this inscription, "To an unknown god." What therefore you worship as unknown, this I proclaim to you. The God who made the world and everything in it, being Lord of heaven and earth, does not live in shrines made by man nor is he served by human hands, as though he needed anything, since he himself gives to all men life and breath and everything. And he made from one, every nation of men to live on all the face of the earth, having determined allotted periods and boundaries of their habitation ... for "In him we live and move and have our being"; as even some of your poets have said, "For we are indeed his offspring."* — Acts 17:22-28

Paul, an unknown apostle, helping Athenians to find, to meet, to encounter an unknown God.

Paul writes: "God has revealed to us through the Spirit. For the Spirit searches everything, even the depths of God" (1 Corinthians 2:10).

Likewise we search for God, and for us God is only partially known and is partially unknown. We need others to help us experience God, our Rock and our Salvation. The One who creates the storm and calms the storm, the One who breathes life into every breast, sets the stars in the heavens and the planets on their course. "No one comprehends the thoughts of God except the Spirit of

90

God. Now we have received not the spirit of the world, but the Spirit which is from God, that we might understand the gifts bestowed on us by God" (1 Corinthians 2:11-12).

Then, too, we serve a Savior, who for a time was unknown to Paul *and who must ever become more real for us.* Even in his own time, the Savior's own people, in his own church, said, "By what authority do you teach?" At his birth, those who were wise came from afar, saying, "Where is he who was born King?" And Herod asked, "Who is he?" When John the Baptizer was at the Jordan, he informed his followers; "There is one who is coming who is mightier than I — the thong of whose sandal I am not worthy to bow down and untie." And John's followers later asked Jesus, "Are you the one or shall we look for another?" Also, the Savior to his own disciples asked, "Who do you say that I am?"

And who among us can claim to know the Savior — fully to know the Savior? We know his story, we have known those who have followed him, we have caught a glimpse of him, for he saved us, and before we could look him straight in the face he was back doing his SAVING work. We have heard his voice and we have answered him. When the Savior makes lunch he breaks the loaves and the fish; when the Savior says arise, even the dead stand up. If he speaks harshly to a tree, it withers or when he speaks kindly to a child, he breathes life. So why is this Savior unknown to us? Because of his great fullness ... and because of our littleness. The Savior is for us, always beyond us and yet with us, always ahead of us and yet leading us, always.

If one visits Arlington National Cemetery in the nation's capital, an important place to pause is The Tomb of the Unknowns. Every thirty minutes there is the solemn ceremony of the changing of the guard. Every detail is checked and with great precision the graves of the unknown are honored and protected. Those who have sacrificed greatly, paid for the blessings of our nation with their lives and who have remained unknown are treated with highest respect.

So it is with those who have sacrificed greatly for our faith. What names, what faces come to mind when you think of how you know God, how our Savior has become known to you, how grace has claimed you, how love and life and hope and joy have become real — which faces? We cannot fathom the mystery of those who come to mind, of the love they have shared, of the ways they spared not themselves, that we might know, that we might live. And by our lives we watch over them, salute them; we kneel, bow, and pray. We stand watch with hearts too full for words, an ineffable glimpse of light which nearly blinds. How many have given, helped, saved, whose names we know not?

Will we likewise be unknown apostles? Will our names ever be written in any volume of history or on a gospel page?

An English gentleman was in this country for a stateside celebration of a wedding which had happened in Britain months earlier. His daughter had married a midwesterner and it seemed fitting to come and get acquainted with the family and friends of his daughter's new husband. Chatting with the groom's childhood pastor, the topic of American churches came up. "Do you know anything about Congregational churches?" he asked the pastor and continued, "I've been doing some research into the history of our home, our house — it's Elizabethan, not Elizabeth II, it was built in 1502. The house is called 'Green Leaves' and discovering its history has really been very difficult. But, as it turns out, in the mid-1800s the Congregational Church was begun in our town in a house called Green Leaves."

"In your home?" the pastor asked, astonished.

"In our home!" the gentleman laughed, still astonished himself.

Let there always be a home for God in us, which God will use to unleash God's power, that we may be God's tools through giving, helping, and saving. And it is important, even as God is at home in us, that we be unknown and partially known apostles remembering that God and the Savior are also partially known. For we do our giving, helping, saving, not for adulation in the eyes of men and women, but for the love of God. While of course it is important that we make known to whom the glory belongs, and also important that we be vital in the knowledge of who drives us as we give, help, and save. More important still is the saving done when we set aside our own glory, for this more truly reflects the example of Jesus.

Recently Andy attended his twenty-fifth class reunion. He had a great time. It was wonderful to see everyone (except for the fellow who still looks like his class picture). Old stories flowed; laughter and music filled the room. Someone pulled out old pictures and school newspapers; good food and friendly teasing were a balm on scrapes and bruises from decades of real world challenges. When the party ended Andy was pleased he had come but haunted by especially one thing — a classmate he had seen was clearly down on his luck. The two had been good friends in school, but where the years had been good to Andy, they had not been good to his friend and it showed. As he walked away from the party, Andy resolved to touch base with his friend from time to time, to keep better track of his friend, to encourage his friend better. Andy decided this as a promise to himself; his friend would never know that the secret pledge had been made ... Is there someone we know today for whom we could make such a pledge, for whom our giving, helping, encouraging might make all the difference?

Will We Be Unknown Apostles?

So will we likewise be unknown apostles? Will our names ever be written in any volume of history or on a gospel page?

If we follow the example of the One who spoke to Paul on the Damascus road,
the One we know only in part but know well enough to be saved by him;
if we follow the One who not only blesses bread but who is the Bread of Life,
who not only offers water but who is Living Water,
if we follow the One who not only drinks of life's bitter cup but who provides for us, becomes for us the Cup of Wonder,

we will often become
unknown apostles,
blessing others before they know it,
healing before the hurt,
lifting before the fall,
named only in the heart of heaven.

Moving At The Speed Of Light:
On The Mountain

Peter 1:16-21

Peter went to the mountain with Jesus. And what happened there was of such magnitude that decades after the resurrection, it still was of bedrock importance to Peter's witness for Christ. We know the story. Peter and James and John went with Jesus up to a high place, apart from the others. And while they were there Jesus' appearance before them changed. They saw him stand with Moses and Elijah. As Matthew describes, "His face shown like the sun, and his garments became white as light." Peter offered to make shelters for each one, for Moses, for Elijah, and for Jesus. What a compliment, placing Jesus on an even plain with two of Israel's most revered and faithful fathers. But Peter's comments were swept away by the coming of a sudden bright cloud. "*This* is my beloved Son, with whom I am well pleased," the voice of God — a moment of divine clarification for all eternity, and Peter was privileged to hear it. No wonder this time on the mountain with Jesus was bedrock for Peter's witness. From then on, as they came down from the mountain and wherever they went, they saw only Jesus.

We all go to the mountain. Sometimes we go for inspiration, or solitude, or adventure. Sometimes we go because we must travel over the mountain or through the mountains because our life journey requires it. But it is certain that on the mountain we will find a place which is challenging, mysterious, perplexing, often threatening, exhausting, and sometimes unforgiving.

Taking The Elephants Over The Mountains.
Hannibal was the son of a general around 220 B.C. in the days of the Roman Empire. His father, a Carthaginian officer, trained

95

the young Hannibal to disdain the Romans. Later, after Hannibal's commander was assassinated, Hannibal, at age 26, was named commander in chief by the acclamation of those under his command. The Carthaginian leadership quickly affirmed the field promotion. Hannibal strengthened his armies until they were ready to confront Rome. Leaving Spain with approximately 40,000 troops, horsemen, and 38 elephants, he made his way through southern France (Gaul) and prepared to enter Italy from the north over the Alps.

We remember Hannibal as the one who took the elephants over the mountains, but few remember the challenges he faced along the way. First the river. He crossed the Rhône using commandeered boats for his troops, and for the elephants, he built earth-covered rafts. But how would they find their way in the Alps? Some friendly, local Gallic leaders assigned guides to help with the complicated Alpine passes, but many Alpine natives were hostile. As Hannibal and his ten thousands threaded the precipitous mountain paths, local residents rolled heavy stones down upon man and beast from the heights above. His descent on an icy base covered with fresh snow caused animals and soldiers to founder, and a landslide blocked their narrow path, delaying progress for a day. After fifteen days crossing the Alps, Hannibal descended into Italy, with 26,000 troops and a few of the original elephants.

So, Hannibal got the elephants over the mountains, with mixed results. For some time he controlled large sections of Italy, but he never reached Rome, and finally was driven from there. Unwelcome at home because of his perceived mismanagement of the Roman campaign, he died a man on the run, pursued by the Romans.[1]

In Every Life There Come Times
To Get The Elephants Over The Mountains

Everyone goes to the mountains. And almost everyone at some-time must take the elephants over the mountains, which is much different than simply going there. By "taking the elephants over the mountains" I mean a grueling, lengthy, nearly back-breaking, dangerous trek for which one is by all appearances only partially prepared. Raising a child, attaining an advanced degree, building a business, facing a long and serious illness or recovering from a devastating accident, facing and recovering from marital difficulty or enduring and healing from divorce, returning to regular living after the death of a loved one, recovery from an addiction — all of these and many more are places in life where we must take the elephants over the mountains. And we take the elephants over the mountains in a final sense when our bodies wind down in this world and we make the transition to the next. It was a part of life for Jesus, it was a part of life for his followers, it is a part of life for Christ's church, and it is a part of life for each one of us.

A seminarian in his thirties has been called to County Hospital. Not long for this world is Blanche, age 57. The chaplain on duty indicates that he doesn't think she has family, but somewhere hospital records show a connection with this student pastor's church. While the pastor does not recognize her name, he will be glad to check on her. The chaplain walks him to Blanche's room, which is on the second floor, and they pause for prayer before the pastor enters. The stench of someone working hard at dying is in the air. The pastor enters unnoticed and he wonders whether Blanche is past responding. The motion on the heart monitor means she is still alive. Beeping from the IV fills the room and the rattle of Blanche's breath rattles the preacher. He has never been around death as a pastor. Eyes open only a slit, Blanche appears mostly asleep. He turns to leave, desiring the easy relief of the hallway. "No," he thinks, "if she can hear me, Blanche needs to know I've come."

"Blanche ... Blanche ... My name is Rudy. I'm the pastor at Mt. Zion." He speaks quietly and close to her ear. Her eyes open a bit. The charge nurse comes in to change the IV bag, which stops the beeping.

"If you want her to hear you, talk loud, right into her ear." Then demonstrating, "BLANCHE, BLANCHE, YOUR PREACHER'S HERE." As Blanche's eyes open, the nurse is called away to another patient's room.

Rudy bends and speaks loudly, "MY NAME IS RUDY. I'M THE PASTOR AT MT. ZION. YOU KNOW, MT. ZION."

Blanche lunges, arms outstretched, in the direction of the pastor with such strength that Rudy straightens up, glancing over his shoulder expecting to see that one of Blanche's friends has come into the room, such was her gesture of bond and kinship.

But no one had come ... except for Rudy in the name of the Church. No one was there except for Rudy, and the One who stood behind him, who stands behind him. In that moment Rudy realized that pastors, and Christians for that matter, are no more than a currency issued by the Kingdom, useful because of the worth of the One who stands behind them.

Blanche was bringing the elephants over the mountains one more time this side of heaven, and she knew that if she could touch even the fringe of his garments she would be healed. She received her healing that night, her eternal healing, touching the fringe of his garments which temporarily had been entrusted to Rudy, who said at her funeral, "Blanche, beloved daughter of our Father, your faith has made you well."

So it is true that in each of our lives in some season we take the elephants over the mountains, and in these times of intensity, sacrifice, danger, and uncertainty, all of our resources are required and the resources of those around us. Often we see Christ clearly on the mountain. And it is also true that, the mountains successfully mastered, we reach a place where we make our descent from the lofty places to the plain. And if the journey has been difficult, which taking the elephants over the mountains inevitably is, we come to rest upon the plain, changed. And when we come from the mountain to the plain, our descending approach can make all the difference.

The couple has just dropped off their son to begin college. A mom sits with her husband in a diner. One hundred fifty miles ago they were setting their eighteen-year-old up in his dorm room. Now they sip their coffee with not much to say. They will drive another 200 miles tonight, but for now they are pensive over supper. She has turned her boy loose to try life on his own and wonders if she has taught him enough or taught him the right things. A mixture of excitement, loss, and fear have taken away her appetite. Proud that she didn't make a good-bye scene, she is doing a little better than expected, which is good because in less than a week she will be sending off to college another eighteen-year-old and a twenty-year-old. Things lately have been so lively in the house, now they will be much more quiet. She used to wish that once in a while it would be more *quiet.*

A few tables away two tired parents preside over a noisy table. Just the two of them and three children in high chairs. At first she notices the noisy five with an uncomprehending stare, but then her eyes grow pink and she reaches for a Kleenex.

"Look, Honey, over there," she says nodding to the trio of high chairs, "that was us sixteen years ago."

The coffee cups emptied, her husband heads for the cashier, while his wife stops at the noisy table.

"We had three in high chairs, same as you. It's tiring, isn't it? We're sending our three off to college this fall. Take time to enjoy them." She pats the hand of the tired mother. "We're going home to a house that will be a little too quiet."

So, they got the elephants over the mountains, having struggled and sacrificed for years, and now the children are on their own and their parents are on their own. How will it be living in a too quiet home? How will these two spend their time? Where will the joy come from, the reason for being? The elephants are over the mountains and how will life be now? So the mountain successfully mastered, we reach a place where we make our descent from the lofty places to the plain. And when the journey has been difficult, we come to rest upon the plain, changed.

When We Come From The Mountain To The Plain, Our Descending Approach Can Make All The Difference

When Hannibal came down from the mountains to the plain of northern Italy, he expected to find there the enemy. And the enemy he did find: endless struggle, conflict, eventual defeat — he was driven from that place.

A temptation for us is to think that taking the elephants over the mountains will leave us the same — unchanged. And that simply we need to arrive upon the plain and be on our way, which is never the case. We can, however, plot a new course and travel the plain differently and successfully.

But there are a few things to keep in mind. When Peter, James, and John came down from the mountain, they saw only Jesus, which meant that their view of everything else had changed. Eventually Peter's ministry took him far and wide to unfamiliar places and people. When we come down from the mountain, *learn the terrain*. Learn in a new way the interests, the appetites, the gifts, of those around us and the special opportunities afforded by this location. Thoreau reminds us that the entire world may be seen in a few acres of ground if we will only see. So *learn the terrain*.

Secondly: *say "yes" to the plain*. Hannibal came down from the mountain and expected to find the enemy, and he found strife and conflict, misery and defeat. Peter, James, and John came down from the mountain and saw Jesus only. When we in our life journey have taken the elephants over the mountains, who will we be and where will we find joy? Whom will we see? Whom will we expect to meet on the plain? Will we be ready to receive the treasures of a new place? Will we be ready to receive the blessings which are ours to receive as changed people? Will we patiently and gently come to know the worth of those we meet who are differently gifted than ourselves? And will we be free in an unexpected place to touch the fringe of his garment?

From the lofty places to the plain, our descending approach can make all the difference. And Jesus, who Peter, James, and John saw differently on the mountain, after the Resurrection said to his disciples, ***"I am going ahead of you and I will meet you on the plain."***

---

1. "Hannibal," *The Encyclopedia Britannica*, 1993 edition, vol. 5, pp. 683 - 685.

Books In This Cycle A Series

GOSPEL SET
And Then Came The Angel
Sermons for Advent/Christmas/Epiphany
William B. Kincaid, III

The Lord Is Risen! He Is Risen Indeed! He Really Is!
Sermons For Lent/Easter
Richard L. Sheffield

No Post-Easter Slump
Sermons For Sundays After Pentecost (First Third)
Wayne H. Keller

We Walk By Faith
Sermons For Sundays After Pentecost (Middle Third)
Richard Gribble

Where Gratitude Abounds
Sermons For Sundays After Pentecost (Last Third)
Joseph M. Freeman

FIRST LESSON SET
Between Gloom And Glory
Sermons For Advent/Christmas/Epiphany
R. Glen Miles

Cross, Resurrection, And Ascension
Sermons For Lent/Easter
Richard Gribble

Is Anything Too Wonderful For The Lord?
Sermons For Sundays After Pentecost (First Third)
Leonard W. Mann

The Divine Salvage
Sermons For Sundays After Pentecost (Middle Third)
R. Curtis and Tempe Fussell

When God Says, "Let Me Alone"
Sermons For Sundays After Pentecost (Last Third)
William A. Jones

SECOND LESSON SET
Moving At The Speed Of Light
Sermons For Advent/Christmas/Epiphany
Frank Luchsinger

Love Is Your Disguise
Sermons For Lent/Easter
Frank Luchsinger